Simple Knitting

a how-to-knit workshop with 20 desirable projects

Erika Knight

photography by
Yuki Sugiura

Quadrille
PUBLISHING

Editorial director Jane O'Shea
Creative director Helen Lewis
Project editor Lisa Pendreigh
Pattern checker Gina Alton
Designer Claire Peters
Photographer Yuki Sugiura
Stylist Charis White
Illustrator Claire Peters
Production director Vincent Smith
Production controller Ruth Deary

First published in 2010 by
Quadrille Publishing Ltd
Alhambra House
27–31 Charing Cross Road
London WC2H 0LS
www.quadrille.co.uk

Text and project designs
© 2010 Erika Knight
Photography
© 2010 Yuki Sugiura
Artwork, design and layout
© 2010 Quadrille Publishing Ltd

The rights of Erika Knight to be identified as
the author of this work have been asserted by
her in accordance with the Copyright, Design,
and Patents Act 1988.

British Library Cataloguing-in-Publication Data
A catalogue record for this book is available
from the British Library.

ISBN: 978 184400 815 5

Printed in China

Knitting fascinates me. Possibly, this is because it is a simple craft that anyone can master. All you need are two sticks and a continuous thread then, by making a series of interlocking loops, you can create textiles that are both practical and decorative. I find the process of knitting greatly inspiring and never tire of the endless variations and forms its practise may take.

I want to share the simplicity of knitting with you. This book is not an exhaustive encyclopaedic how-to-knit tome, instead I have pared down the craft to the essential knitting basics as I see them. For example, I haven't included every possible way to cast on stitches (at the last count, there were twenty-two), instead I believe in mastering just the few ways that are easy, effective and give the right look I am seeking for a specific design. *Simple Knitting* is knitting my style. In this book I have aimed to provide the basic means to get you knitting – it can be as easy as 'in, over, under, off.'

In the Materials & Techniques section at the start of this book, I have set out the technical how-to information for the basic knitting methods, but knowing how to work a particular technique is no use in isolation and really only makes sense once it is put into practice. This is where the Project Workshops come in. In fact, providing you can master the simple techniques of casting on, casting off and working the knit stitch, you can easily make the first few items in the Project Workshops section of this book. There are twenty projects in all, from 'getting started' mufflers, thrifty 'stitch-practising' dishcloths and contemporary fold-over cushions, each suitable for the beginner knitter, to more challenging short-row shaping socks, colour-blocked blankets and a vintage-inspired intarsia rose tea cosy.

Each project provides the opportunity to practise a technique or two by way of a masterclass. It's up to you whether you want to work your way through the projects sequentially, gathering a little momentum with each masterclass, or dip into the projects here and there, practising and perfecting a specific technique.

Soon you will become adept at shaping by increasing, decreasing and short-row shaping, twisting stitches to form cables and plaits and changing colours through striping, stranding and colour blocking.

The variety of projects in *Simple Knitting* very much reflects my personal preference for a pared-down style; simple shapes generally with little decoration in which the texture and shade of each yarn – natural fibres and muted colour tones – are integral to my designs. I am, however, exacting about how I make up the final piece: it is essential to take the time to finish a project. But again this is easy; since someone showed me invisible seaming and I seldom use anything else. I share this with you. I've also added a few helpful design tips here and there as notes in the margins, just as I would in my own sketch- and workbooks. I hope they help to gain you an insight into how I approach knitwear design.

As well as honing the skills given in the Materials & Techniques section and practised in the Project Workshops, I hope you will also enjoy the variety of textures that can be created with knitting. I have included twenty of my very favourite stitches alongside some simple tried-and-tested colourways in the Stitch Library. I hope that they will inspire you to try out different stitch textures and play with colours in order to forge ahead to create your own style.

This book, *Simple Knitting*, is very much my take on the craft. I love the entire process of creating and constructing a knitted fabric. I hope that you will share my love for the craft and, within these pages, find the inspiration to pick up those sticks and, well, just get knitting.

Skill levels

BEGINNER

1 Beginner Projects for first-time knitters using basic knit and purl stitches. Minimal shaping.

EASY

2 Easy Projects using basic stitches, repetitive stitch patterns, simple colour changes and simple shaping and finishing.

INTERMEDIATE

3 Intermediate Projects with a variety of stitches, such as basic cables and lace, simple intarsia, double-pointed needle and knitting in the round needle techniques, mid-level shaping and finishing.

EXPERIENCED

4 Experienced Projects using advanced techniques and stitches, such as short rows, fair isle, more intricate intarsia, cables, lace patterns and numerous colour changes.

materials and techniques

Choosing yarns and colours

Due to my many years working within the fashion industry, the selection of materials is paramount to me when designing hand knits; very often it is the yarn or indeed the fibre that is the starting point for a project.

I take a lot of time and care to ensure that the fibre, the yarn, the stitch, the weight of the knitted fabric and the detailing are just right for the proposed design. I believe the time taken over this really pays off, so I always knit up a large swatch of the yarn and ask myself a series of questions. Are the fibres as soft to the touch as I would like? Does the yarn give good stitch clarity? Is the knitted fabric too heavy or too light? Is the yarn and resulting fabric fit for the purpose for which it is intended? Does the overall effect match up to my original design idea? All these questions are especially important, even when designing a seemingly simple piece like the Muffler (see pages 64–7) or the Fold-over cushion (see pages 70–3).

In fact, the success of a simple design more often than not hinges on the quality of the yarn selected. In the case of the pair of cushions shown together on pages 71 and 72, the contrasting matte mohair and sheeny silk fabrics team up to give these cushions a sumptuous and luxurious feel. The high-quality natural fibre I have used for the pure silk cushion takes the dye colour well and when knitted up creates a fabric that drapes beautifully, whilst the whisper-fine mohair yarn has an airy, ethereal texture that juxtaposes the smoother silk.

I tend to use natural yarns because of the inherent characteristics of their fibres – they keep the wearer warm in winter yet cool in summer, wicking moisture away from the skin. Moreover natural fibres are light, soft, comfortable to wear and not without the hint of luxury that comes only from wearing nature's finest – after all nature does it best!

For the projects in this book, I have chosen a variety of yarns for their unique textures. Primarily, I have selected animal fibres, including the softest baby alpaca, robust extra-fine merino wool, rare British sheeps breed wool and voluminous light-weight wools, as well as refined silks and diaphanous mohair. Alongside these luxurious animal fibres, sit a small selection of the best natural plant fibres: the versatile staple, organic cotton, and the most ancient of the plant fibres, the exquisite linen.

Whether designing hand-knit garments or homewares, I lean towards an understated colour palette of muted tones. Preferring to use the characteristic colours of the natural yarns as a base, I usually introduce stronger 'fashion' or seasonal colours only as highlights within the overall scheme. Somehow this just seems like second nature to me now when putting together a colour story, hence I return time and time again to my favourite palette of pale milk, oyster and pearl, rose pink, mouse and taupe, misty and smoky blues, inky carbon and the deepest peat brown, with chartreuse and willow supplying little touches of colourful relief.

I love to put opposites together, whether they be colour or texture. Natural yarns create an exciting contrast when placed against man-made materials, for example smooth, extra-fine merino wool draped across cool glass or flat, matte cotton cast over highly polished concrete can give vitality and textural interest to the home.

Often a cherished, inherited or found piece of furniture may be the starting point for a project. A favourite worn leather couch deserves a cosy throw, an ageing dining chair begs a comfortable cushion – these things can often be my inspiration. Whatever you wish to create and make, whether it is for you to wear or to accessorise your home, within these pages I hope you may find yarns, stitches, designs, techniques, tips and even colour palettes to inspire you too.

Yarns: fine

Fine yarns offer some of the most refined and delicate materials to knit with – from gossamer thin mohair to sumptuous cashmere, from hand-dyed silk to paper-feel cotton. Although knitting with fine yarn may be a little more time consuming, the end result is an especially rewarding neat fabric with a clearly defined stitch.
Fine yarn textiles often look less 'handmade', more closely resembling a machine woven fabric with a professional finish.

Opposite (clockwise from top left) A mohair and silk blend yarn (Rowan Kidsilk Haze); a pure silk yarn (Alchemy Silken Straw); a mohair and silk blend yarn (Rowan Kidsilk Haze); a pure silk yarn, which feels like linen (Habu Silk Gima); a pure cashmere yarn (Habu Naturally Dyed Cashmere); a pure cotton yarn, which feels like paper (Habu Cotton Gima)

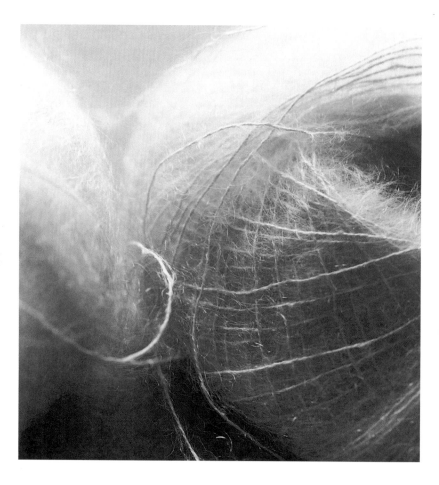

 Yarn weight: super fine
4-ply, sock, baby
Average knitted tension: 27–32 stitches
Recommended needle size (metric): 2.25–3.25mm
Recommended needle size (imperial): 1–2

 Yarn weight: fine
light-weight dk, baby
Average knitted tension: 23–26 stitches
Recommended needle size (metric): 3.25–3.75mm
Recommended needle size (imperial): 3–5

(These are the most commonly used tensions and needle sizes for these yarn categories.)

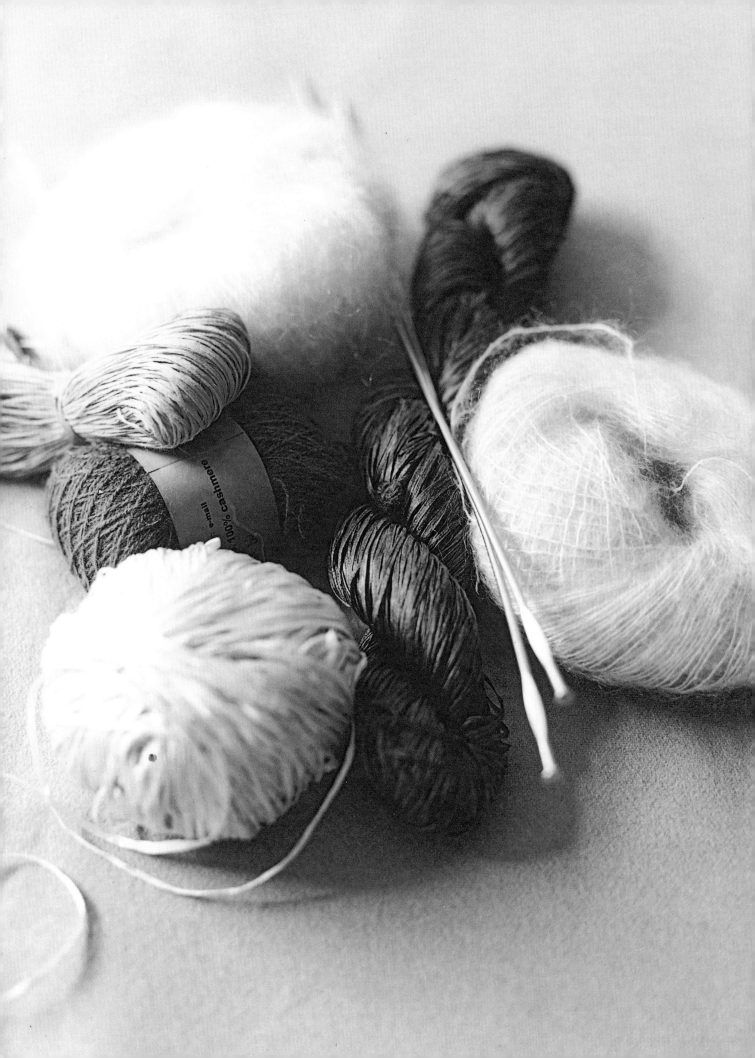

Yarns: medium

Medium is the most popular of all yarn weights as it is both easy to source and to knit with. This category of yarns includes a vast array of fibres – I favour pure fibres and blends – and textures, ranging from smooth matte cottons and linens to naturally marled rare sheeps breed wools. As spinners generally offer a wider palette of colours in medium weight yarns, I tend to use standard double-knitting yarns for my more colourful designs.

 Yarn weight: light
dk
Average knitted tension: 21–24 stitches
Recommended needle size (metric): 3.75–4.5mm
Recommended needle size (imperial): 5–7

 Yarn weight: medium
aran
Average knitted tension: 16–20 stitches
Recommended needle size (metric): 4.5–5.5mm
Recommended needle size (imperial): 7–9

(These are the most commonly used tensions and needle sizes for these yarn categories.)

Opposite (clockwise from top left) A linen blend yarn (Rowan Lenpur Linen); a pure alpaca yarn (Rowan Baby Alpaca DK); a pure wool yarn (Rowan Purelife British Sheeps Breeds DK Undyed); a pure cotton yarn (Rowan Purelife Organic Cotton DK Naturally Dyed); a mohair and silk blend yarn (Rowan Kidsilk Aura); a linen blend yarn (Rowan Lenpur Linen); a pure cotton yarn (Rowan Purelife Organic Cotton DK Naturally Dyed)

Yarns: fat

Bulky yarns – or fat yarns as I call them – are some of my favourites. Their sheer volume is inspirational. By bulky I am referring to yarns over double-knitting weight, including aran, chunky, bulky and the now-legendary big wool. It's great to learn to knit with bulky weight yarn on big needles as you're able to see the stitches very clearly and, of course, as the knitting grows very quickly it is instantly rewarding. I like to use big yarns for statement projects for the home, such as cushions and throws, where the scale of the yarn adds a certain homespun fun to couches and chairs.

Opposite (clockwise from top left) A wool blend yarn (Rowan Little Big Wool); a wool-alpaca blend yarn (Blue Sky Alpacas Bulky); a pure cotton yarn made from strips of shirting; a wool-cashmere blend yarn (Debbie Bliss Como); a merino blend yarn (Gedifra Merino Grande)

 **Yarn weight: bulky**
chunky
Average knitted tension: 12–15 stitches
Recommended needle size (metric): 5.5–8mm
Recommended needle size (imperial): 9–11

6 **Yarn weight: super bulky**
super chunky
Average knitted tension: 6–11 stitches
Recommended needle size (metric):
8mm and larger
Recommended needle size (imperial):
11 and larger

(These are the most commonly used tensions and needle sizes for this yarn category.)

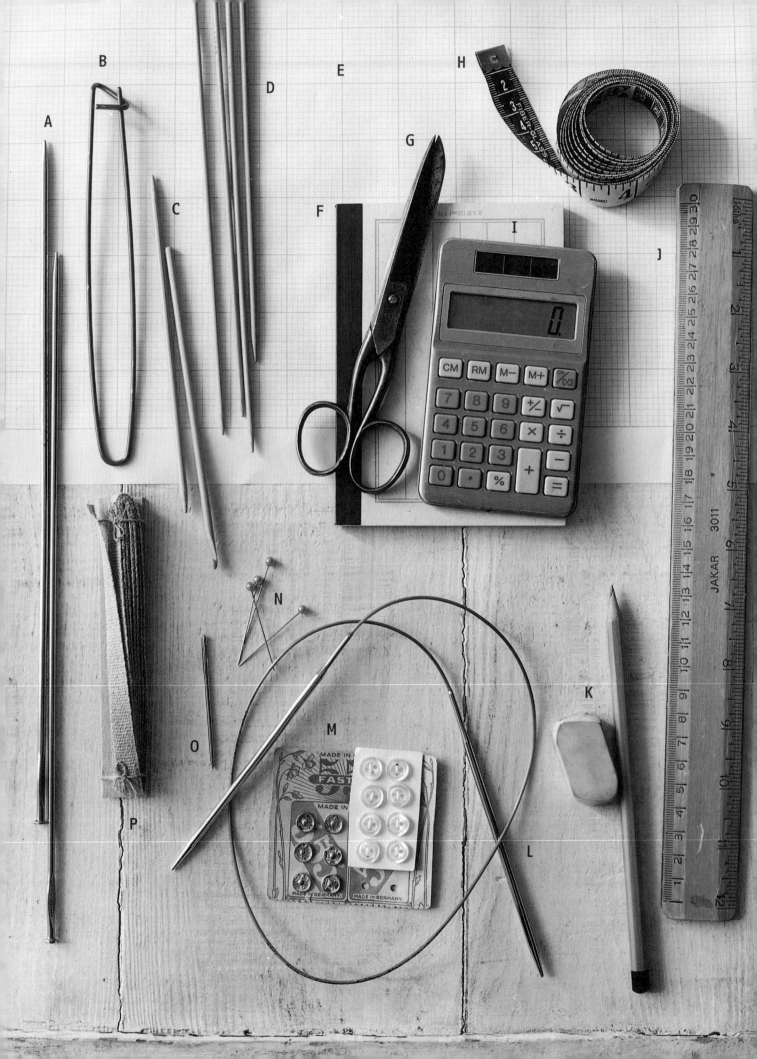

Equipment

A pair of sticks and a continuous length of yarn is all you need to start knitting. Sticks, or rather knitting needles or pins, come in various sizes from fine to fat, in sets of two or four, and attached to wires. There are certain other pieces of equipment that can make the knitting process that little bit easier. Here are some of the most common, and most useful...

A straight pins: my personal preference in knitting needles is for bamboo, but there is also metal, wood, plastic and vintage tortoiseshell to choose from; sizes range from fine to fat, most popularly from 2.75mm through to 15mm. Sizes differ in the US from the UK (see page 143 for a conversion chart)

B stitch holder: for keeping a set of stitches secure and preventing them from unravelling whilst they are not being worked; you can also use large safety pins

C crochet hook: for picking up dropped stitches or adding crochet edges to projects

D set of four double-pointed needles: for working stitches in the round to create a seamless piece of knitting; gaining popularity are square needles (see page 34)

E graph paper: for working out small motifs or drawing out shapings in pattern instructions

F notebook: for recording all those stitch counts and any pattern amendments; we always think that we'll remember them, but then forget them when we come to knit the design again

G scissors: for snipping yarns and cutting fabrics and trims

H tape measure: for checking dimensions; make sure the tape is not too old or stretched and always measure on a flat surface

I calculator: for working out tensions, especially when using a different yarn to the one specified in a pattern, or calculating stitch and row counts when creating your own design

J ruler: for accurately measuring a tension swatch; a ruler is better than a tape measure because of its straight, flat edge

K pencil and eraser: for recording any notes and amendments in your notebook or directly onto your pattern as you knit, and for amending your amendments

L circular pin or 'wire': primarily for working in the round, like double-pointed needles, however many knitters prefer to use a wire when knitting throws or other large items as the weight of the knitting can rest on the wire in your lap rather on each needle (see page 35)

M press studs and buttons: button styles are a personal preference; classic mother of pearl in either natural cream or natural grey is a favourite of mine as I find it complements almost every yarn shade. To avoid making buttonholes, I often use press studs as the fastening and top with a decorative button. This is a particularly good idea for baby garments

N glass headed pins: for pinning together pieces of knitting; coloured heads enable you to find a pin again when sewing up

O blunt-ended sewing needle: for sewing up finished pieces of knitting and weaving in yarn ends; the needle's large eye makes it easier to thread with bulky yarn

P cotton tape: for trimming a seam; use on the inside of a back neck to make a great finishing detail and to prevent stretching (see page 81)

Holding the yarn and needles

Holding the yarn and knitting needles is possibly the most tricky thing to master when learning to knit. The position you adopt will depend on which of the two basic methods you choose. If you opt for the English method, the yarn is held in your right hand. With the Continental method, the yarn is held in your left. It will take a while to work out which method is right for you. I recommend adopting whichever way you find easiest to achieve a flowing, even tension. Everyone knits slightly differently – for example, some knitters find it easier to work the stitches close to the tip of the needles, whilst others prefer to knit further back on the shafts. Once you find a comfortable knitting position, your speed will increase and your tension will become more regular.

Continental method

Hold the needle with the stitches in your right hand. Wrap the yarn around your little finger and then around the index finger of your left hand. Move the needle holding the stitches into your left hand. With the working needle in your right hand, control the tension of the yarn with your left index finger.

English method

1 Hold the needle with the stitches in your left hand. With the palm of your right hand facing you, wrap the yarn around your little finger, over the other fingers and then underneath the index finger.

2 With the working needle in your right hand, control the tension of the yarn with your right index finger.
OR
An alternate way of holding the working needle is to place in the crook between thumb and index finger as though holding a pencil.

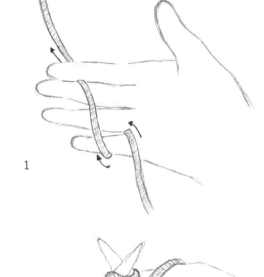

1

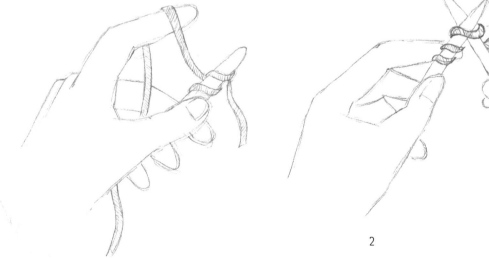

2

Making a slip knot

Before you begin to knit, you must make a
foundation row called a cast on. The first stitch
of any cast-on method is a slip knot. There
are several methods of casting on. The two
examples I give on the following pages are
the ones I believe are the most popular, the
thumb method and the cable method. The thumb
method is a double cast-on technique; for this
you must leave a predetermined length of yarn
free before working the slip knot. A good rule
of thumb is to allow a length of approximately
three times the planned width of the cast-on
edge or 2.5cm per stitch plus a little extra for
insurance. For the thumb method, only a 20–
25cm length of yarn is necessary.

1 Making sure you have left the correct length
of yarn, cross over the strands of yarn to make
a loop.

2 Pull the strand attached to the ball (known as
the working yarn) through the loop to form a
second loop.

3 Place the new loop on the knitting needle.
Tighten this loop on the needle by pulling on
both ends of the yarn. You have formed a slip
knit and are now ready to begin one of the cast-
on methods on the following pages.

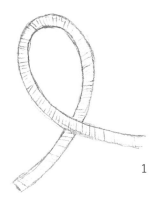

1

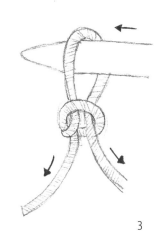

2

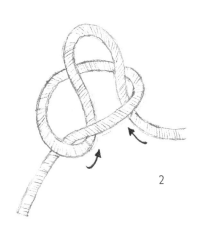

3

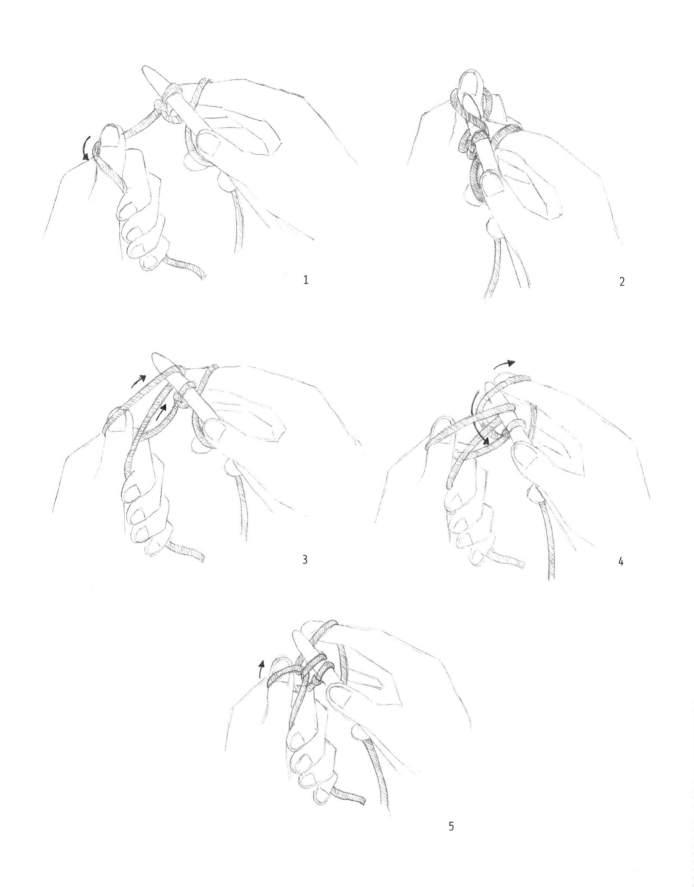

1

2

3

4

5

Casting on

As I have already mentioned, there are over twenty different methods of casting on, but in my opinion you only need the two given here. Each cast on gives a different visual effect and has different properties; the cable cast on is more elastic and so is good for edges where you need a bit of give, such as the hats on pages 90–3, whereas the double cast on is neat but gives a firmer edge with less elasticity so is better suited to cushions and throws.

Double cast on – thumb method

Once you have made a slip knot, remembering to leave a long enough length of yarn (see page 21), this simple method of making stitches uses just one knitting needle, a length of yarn and your thumb.

1 Hold the ball end of the yarn along with the knitting needle with the slip knot in your right hand. Take the loose, measured end of the yarn in your left hand and form a loop around your left thumb.

2 Insert the tip of the needle into the loop around your left thumb.

3 With your right hand, wrap the yarn from the ball over the tip of the needle.

4 Pull the needle under and through the loop on your thumb, bringing with it the yarn wrapped around it.

5 Slip the loop off your thumb and gently tighten the stitch by pulling both strands.

Repeat these steps until you have the required number of stitches.

1 Wrap the ball end of the yarn around your left index finger and the measured end around your left thumb. Holding the needle in your right hand, put the tip up through the loop around your thumb.

2 Take it down through the loop around your index finger and then back under the loop on your thumb. Slip your thumb out of its loop, making sure not to drop the loop off the needle. Gently tighten the stitch by pulling both strands.

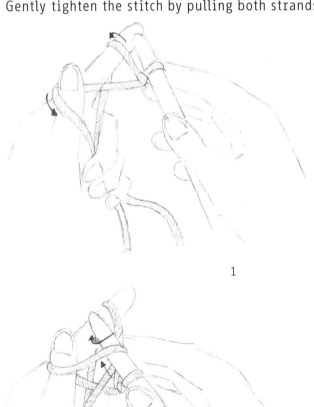

1

2

Cable cast on

The cable cast-on method uses two needles and is particularly good for ribbed edges as it provides a sturdy but still elastic edge. As you need to insert the needle between the stitches and pull the yarn through to create another stitch make sure that you do not make the new stitch too tight. The cable method is one of the most widely used cast ons.

1 Hold the knitting needle with the slip knot in your left hand and insert the tip of the right-hand needle from left to right and from front to back through the slip knot. Wrap the yarn from the ball up and over the tip of the right-hand needle.

2 With the right-hand needle, draw this loop through the slip knot.

3 Do not drop this loop from the left-hand needle.

4 Instead, slip the loop onto the left-hand needle to make a new stitch.

5 Next, insert the right-hand needle between the two stitches on the left-hand needle and wrap the yarn around the tip of the right-hand needle.

6 Draw the loop through. Do not drop this loop from the left-hand needle.

7 Place the loop on the left-hand needle to make a new stitch, as before.

Repeat the steps 5 and 6 until the required number of stitches have been cast on.

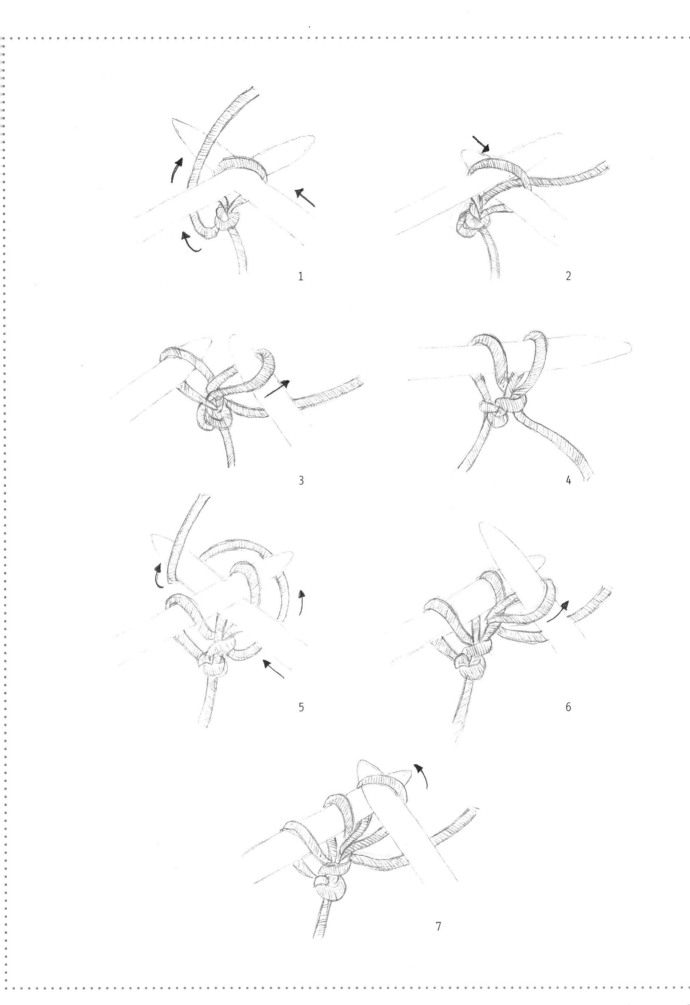

1

2

3

4

5

6

7

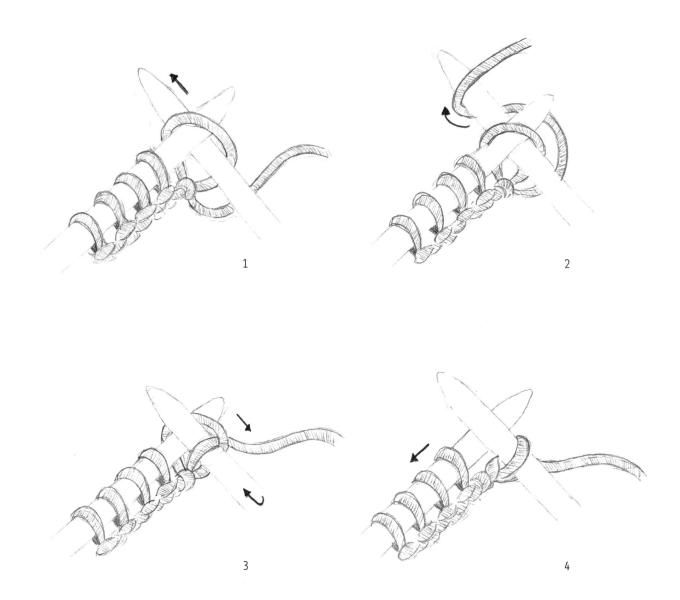

1

2

3

4

Knit one

After casting on the appropriate number of stitches, you can begin to knit your first row. Each stitch is made by the simple four-step process shown here – I always remember it by the chant, 'In, over, under, off'. Each row is completed by repeating this process until all the stitches on the left-hand needle have been transferred to the right-hand needle. Once you have completed each row, switch the needle holding the worked stitches to your left hand and begin again. Another row of knit stitches will create a fabric known as garter stitch (see page 50), but other combinations of stitches will create different textures (see the Stitch Library on pages 48–61).

1 In Hold the needle with the cast-on stitches in your left hand, then holding the other needle in your right hand, insert the tip of the right-hand needle into the first stitch on the left-hand needle. Pass the needle under the loop facing you and up into the centre of the stitch so the needles form an X shape, with the left-hand needle in front of the right-hand needle.

2 Over Holding the working yarn in your right hand, and at the back of the work, wrap the yarn anti-clockwise over the tip of the right-hand needle to make a loop.

3 Under Slide the right-hand needle toward you, passing the tip down and out of the centre of the stitch on the left-hand needle to pull the loop under and through the first stitch on the left-hand needle.

4 Off Slide the original stitch off the tip of the left-hand needle, leaving the new stitch on the right-hand needle. You have now knitted one stitch to the right-hand needle.

Continental method

Hold the needles using the Continental method (see page 20). Put the tip of the right-hand needle into the first stitch on the left-hand needle. Wrap the working yarn in your left hand over the tip of the right-hand needle. Slide the right-hand needle toward you, passing the tip down and out of the centre of the stitch on the left-hand needle to pull the loop under and through the first stitch on the left-hand needle.

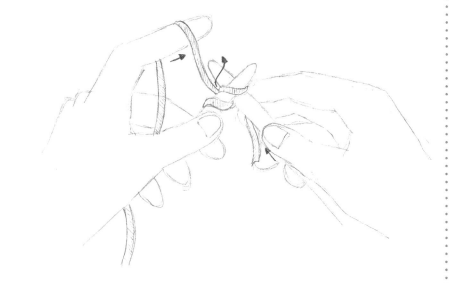

Purl one

This stitch is worked in much the same way as the knit stitch, but with one simple difference: when working the knit stitch, the yarn is held at the back of the work, but with the purl stitch, the yarn is held at the front of the work. Likewise, the purl stitch is made by the simple four-step process shown here. Repeat the process until the row is complete, and all the stitches have been transferred to the right-hand needle. Switch this needle to your left hand before beginning the next row. Combining the knit stitch and the purl stitch provides the basis of all knitted fabrics, including the perennially popular stocking stitch, which is made by working one row knit, one row purl throughout (see page 50). The simple knit stitch and purl stitch is just about all there is to know!

1 In Hold the needle with the cast-on stitches in your left hand. Holding the other needle in your right hand, and with the working yarn at the front of the work, insert the tip of the right-hand needle into the first stitch on the left-hand needle. Pass the needle from back to front through the centre of the first stitch so the needles for an X shape with the right-hand needle in front of the left-hand needle.

2 Over Holding the working yarn in your right hand, and at the front of the work, wrap the yarn anti-clockwise over the point of the right-hand needle to make a loop.

3 Under Slide the right-hand needle back and out of the first stitch on the left-hand needle to pull the loop under and through the first stitch on the left-hand needle.

4 Off Slide the original stitch off the point of the left-hand needle, leaving the new stitch on the right-hand needle. You have now purled one stitch to the right-hand needle.

Continental method

Hold the needles using the Continental method (see page 20), with the yarn to the front of the left-hand needle. Put the tip of the right-hand needle into the first stitch on from back to front. Wrap the working yarn anti-clockwise over the tip of the right-hand needle. Slide the right-hand needle backwards, passing the tip down and out of the centre of the stitch on the left-hand needle to pull the loop under and through the first stitch on the left-hand needle.

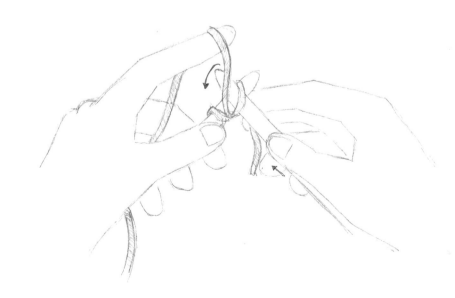

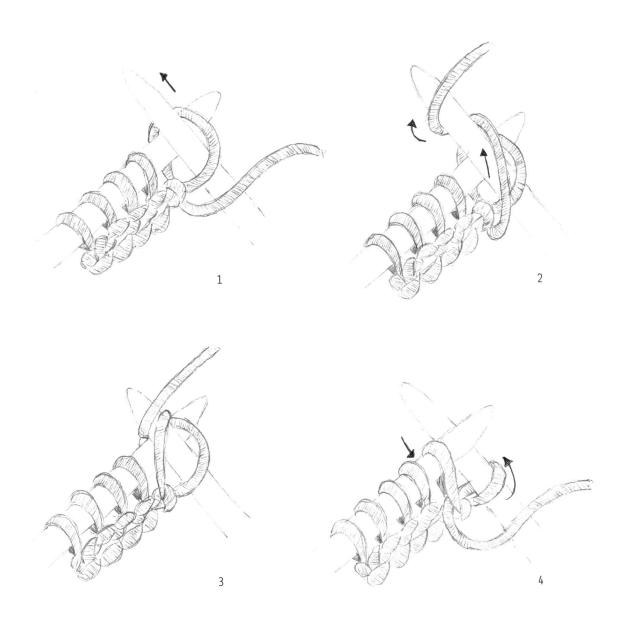

1

2

3

4

Increasing

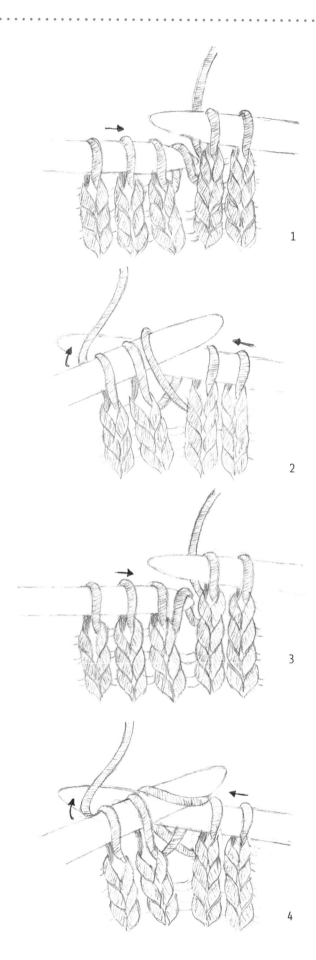

Make one

Adding stitches or taking away stitches – increasing or decreasing – shapes your knitting. There are several methods of increasing, but the simplest way to make an additional stitch is to pick up the horizontal strand that lies between two stitches and knit into the back of it. This type of increase, which is known as 'make one' or 'm1' will slope slightly to the left, however, it is not terribly obvious in the finished piece. For an alternative method, see page 96.

Make one (m1) on a knit row (left sloping)
1 Work to the position of the increase. With the tip of the left-hand needle, lift the horizontal strand that lies between the worked and unworked stitches.

2 Knit into the back of the lifted loop on the left-hand needle to make one new stitch.

Make one (m1) on a knit row (right sloping)
3 Work to the position of the increase. With the tip of the left-hand needle, life the horiztonal strand that lies between the worked and unworked stitches.

4 Knit into the front of the lifted loop on the left-hand needle to make one new stitch.

Decreasing

Take one
The simplest method of taking away stitches, or decreasing, is to knit two stitches together. Knitting the stitches together through the back of the loops forms a left-slanting increase, and knitting through the front of the loops a right-slanting one.

Knit two together (k2tog) (right sloping)
1 Instead of inserting the right-hand needle into one stitch on the left-hand needle, insert the tip into the front of the first two stitches at the same time. Wrap the yarn over the tip of the right-hand needle to make a loop. Slide the right-hand needle toward you, passing the tip down and out of the centre of the two stitches on the left-hand needle to pull the loop through the stitches on the left-hand needle. Slide the original stitches off the left-hand needle in the usual way, making sure that you drop both stitches from the left-hand needle. There is one stitch on the right-hand needle instead of two.

Knit two together through back loop (k2tog tbl) (left sloping)
2 Insert the tip of the right-hand needle into the back of the first two stitches on the left-hand needle. Work in the same way as k2tog, knitting these two stitches together as one.

Purl two together (p2tog) (right sloping)
3 Insert the tip of the right-hand needle into the first two stitches on the left-hand needle from back to front. Purl these two stitches together as one.

Purl two together through back loop (p2tog tbl) (left sloping)
4 Insert the tip of the right-hand needle into the back of the first two stitches on the left-hand needle. Work in the same way as p2tog, purling these two stitches together as one.

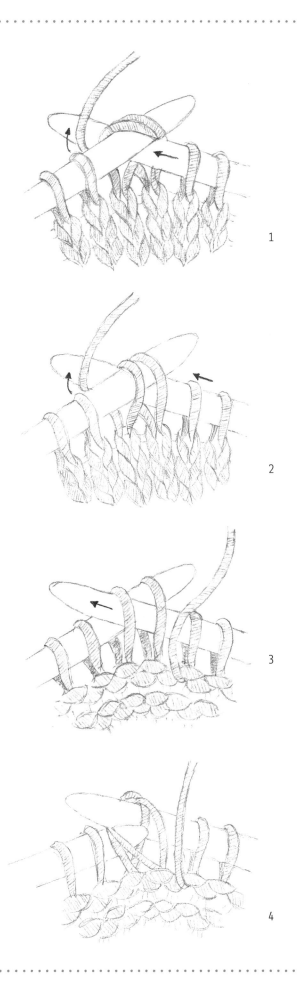

1

2

3

4

Casting off

Basic knit cast off

In most instances this is the very last thing you must to do in order to finish your knitting. It is the process that fixes a piece of knitting so that it does not unravel once taken off the needles.

1 At the beginning of your final row, knit the first two stitches as usual. Insert the tip of the left-hand needle into the front loop of the first knitted stitch on the right-hand needle.

2 Lift the first knitted stitch from the right-hand needle over the second knitted stitch on the right-hand needle.

3 Now remove the left-hand needle so only one knitted stitch remains on the right-hand needle. Knit the next stitch on the left-hand needle, so there are two knitted stitches on the right-hand needle again. Repeat these steps, making sure there are never more than two knitted stitches on the right-hand needle.

Work until one knitted stitch remains on the right-hand needle. Cut the working yarn. Pass the end of the yarn through the last loop. Remove the needle and pull on the end of the yarn to tighten.

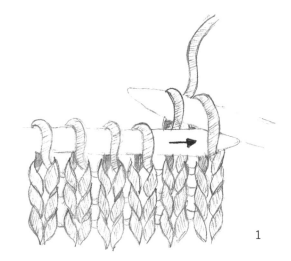

1

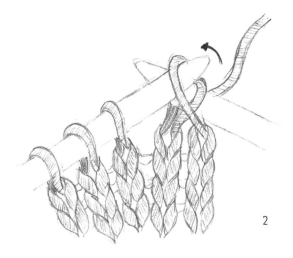

2

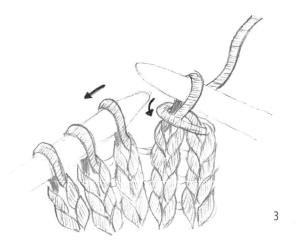

3

Basic purl cast off

The purl cast-off creates a firm edge and is used on purl stitches.

1 At the beginning of your final row, purl the first two stitches as usual. Insert the tip of the left-hand needle from behind the right-hand needle into the back loop of the first purled stitch on the right-hand needle.

2 Lift the first purled stitch from the right-hand needle over the second purled stitch on the right-hand needle.

3 Now remove the left-hand needle so only one purled stitch remains on the right-hand needle. Purl the next stitch on the left-hand needle so there are two purled stitches on the right-hand needle again. Repeat these steps, making sure there are never more than two purled stitches on the right-hand needle.

Work until one purled stitch remains on the right-hand needle. Cut the working yarn. Pass the end of the yarn through the last loop. Remove the needle and pull on the end of the yarn to tighten.

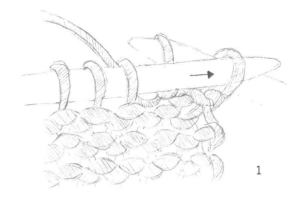

1

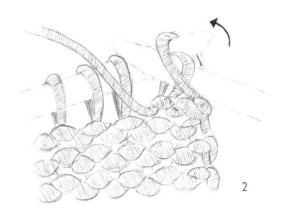

2

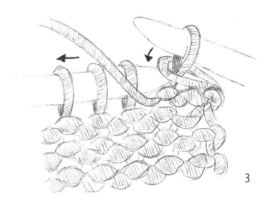

3

Knitting in the round

Knitting in the round can be done on either circular needles or on a set of double-pointed needles. When knitting in the round, the work is joined to make a tubular piece that has no side seams so it is perfect for items such as socks (see pages 110–13). Another advantage is that you only ever work the right side of the fabric, making shaping neater and easier.

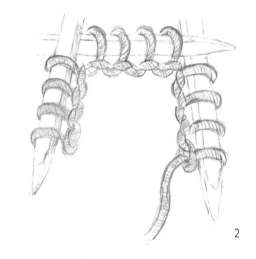

1

Knitting on double-pointed needles

Double-pointed needles have, not surprisingly, points at both ends and come in sets of four or five needles in 18cm and 25cm lengths. It is now possible to get 'square' needles, which are faceted on four sides as opposed to a smooth cylindrical barrel. Some knitters have reported that these 'square' needles help them to achieve a more even tension and reduce any stresses and strains.

1 Cast on the required number of stitches on the first needle, plus one extra. Slip this extra stitch to the next needle as shown. Continue in this way, casting on the required number of stitches on the last needle.

2

2 Arrange the needles as shown, with the cast-on edge facing the centre of the triangle (or square) of stitches.

3 Place a stitch marker or coloured thread after the last cast-on stitch to indicate the end of the round. With the free needle, knit the first cast-on stitch, pulling the yarn tight to avoid a gap. Work in a round until you reach the stitch marker. This completes the first round. Slip the marker to the right-hand needle and work the next round.

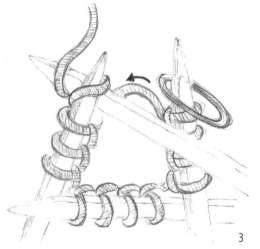

3

Knitting on circular needles (wire)

Circular needles are available in several lengths. The length used depends on the number of stitches you are working with and the tension. The needle should be short enough so that the stitches are not stretched when joined.

Circular needles are available with plastic, aluminium or teflon-coated tips, but all have plastic joining wires. If the plastic wire portion of the needle curls, immerse it in hot water to straighten it before you begin to knit. When you join your work, make sure that the stitches are not twisted around the needle. A twisted cast-on can't be rectified once you have worked a round. To help you keep the stitches untwisted, keep the cast-on edge facing the centre, or work one row before joining the stitches, then sew the gap closed later.

To identify the beginning of each new round, place a marker or differently coloured thread between the first and last cast-on stitches before joining. Slip the marker before each subsequent round.

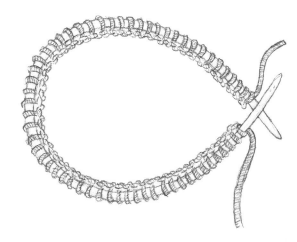

Cast on as you would for straight knitting. Distribute the stitches evenly around the needle, making sure not to twist them. Place a stitch marker or coloured thread after the last cast-on stitch to indicate the end of the round. Hold the needle tip with the last cast-on stitch in your right hand and the tip with the first cast-on stitch in your left hand. Knit the first cast-on stitch, pulling the yarn tight to avoid a gap. Work in a round until you reach the stitch marker. This completes the first round. Slip the marker to the right-hand needle and work the next round.

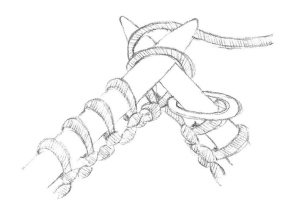

Making a tension swatch

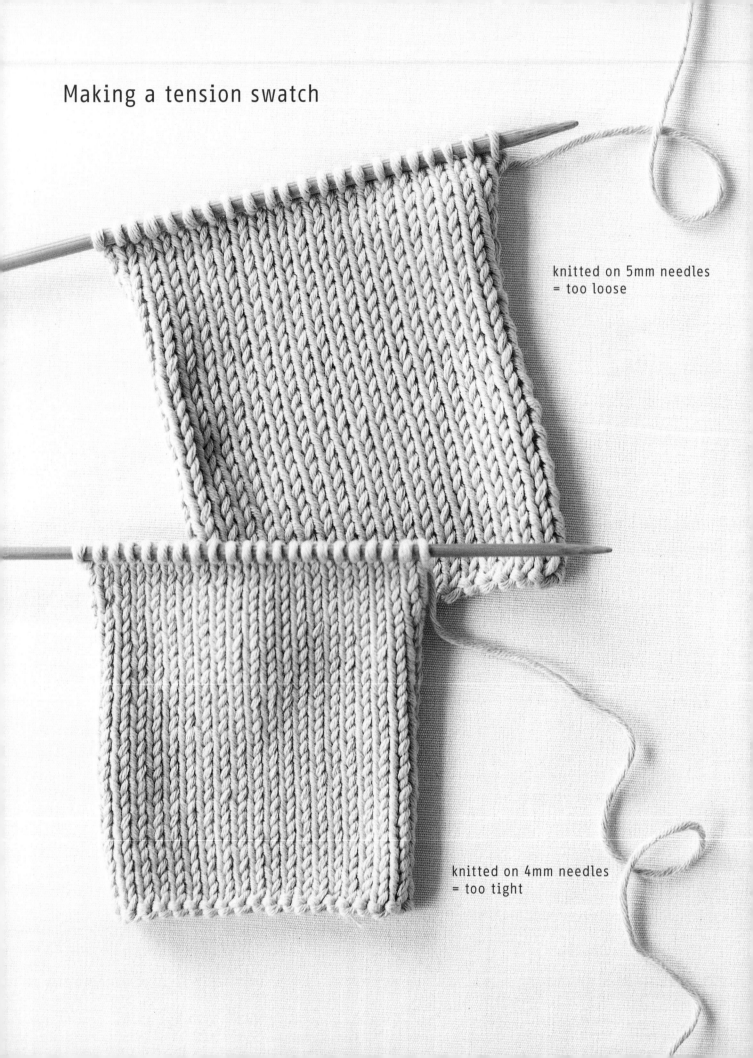

knitted on 5mm needles
= too loose

knitted on 4mm needles
= too tight

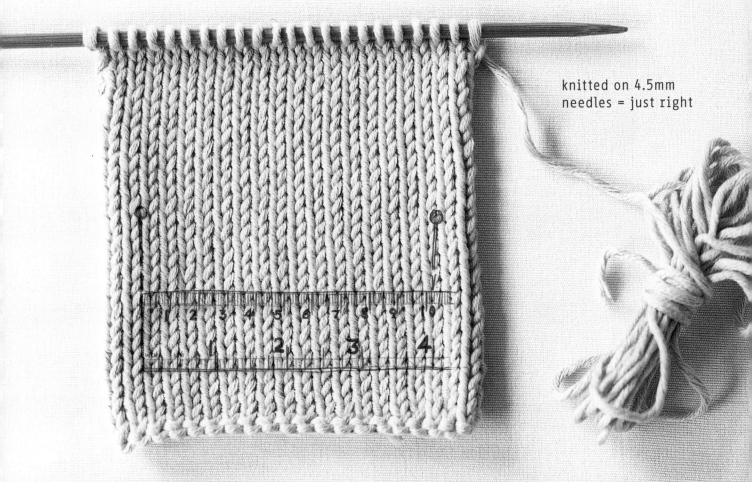

knitted on 4.5mm
needles = just right

It is crucial to check your tension before you embark on any project. Tension is the number of stitches and rows to a centimetre and is also known as the stitch gauge. The tension determines the measurements of a garment, so it is critical you obtain the same number of rows and stitches as the pattern states.

A small difference over 10cm can add up to a considerable amount over the complete width of the knitted garment. If your tension is looser or tighter than the one stated in the knitting pattern, your garment will be larger or smaller than the specified size. So taking time out for 15 minutes to work a tension square before you start can save a lot of heartache later on.

The size of the stitch depends on the yarn, the size of the knitting needles and your control of the yarn. It can also depend on mood - many knitters will have experienced a tighter tension when stress levels are high!

Using the same yarn and needles and stitch that the tension has been measured over in the pattern, knit a sample at least 13cm square.

Measuring a tension swatch

Smooth out the square on a flat surface. To check stitch tension, place a ruler (a cloth tape measure can be less accurate) horizontally on the fabric and mark 10cm with pins. Count the number of stitches between the pins. To check row tension, place a ruler vertically, mark 10cm with pins and count the number of rows. If the number of stitches and rows is greater than it says in the pattern, your tension is higher. This can usually be regulated by using larger needles. If the number of stitches is fewer than the specified number, your tension is looser and you should change to smaller needles. A word of caution: your tension may change from that of your sample when knitting the actual garment, as your knitting can alter when working across more stitches.

Abbreviations

Following is a list of the most commonly used abbreviations within knitting patterns. In addition, special abbreviations may also be included at the start of a pattern, such as the directions for a specific cable stitch, which are not necessarily on this list. Generally, definitions of any special abbreviations used are given at the beginning of a book or pattern.

[ ]	work instructions within square brackets as many times as directed
( )	work instructions within round brackets in the place directed
* *	repeat instructions following the asterisks as directed
*	repeat instructions following the single asterisk as directed
alt	alternate
approx	approximately
beg	begin/beginning
bet	between
C4B	cable four back – slip next 2 stitches onto cable needle and hold at back of work, knit 2 stitches, then knit 2 stitches from cable needle
C4F	cable four forward – slip next 2 stitches onto cable needle and hold at front of work, knit 2 stitches, then knit 2 stitches from cable needle
C8B	cable eight back – slip next 4 stitches onto cable needle and hold at back of work, knit 4 stitches, then knit 4 stitches from cable needle
C8F	cable eight forward – slip next 4 stitches onto cable needle and hold at front of work, knit 4 stitches, then knit 4 stitches from cable needle
C12B	cable twelve back – slip next 6 stitches onto cable needle and hold at back of work, knit 6 stitches, then knit 6 stitches from cable needle
C12F	cable twelve forward – slip next 6 stitches onto cable needle and hold at front of work, knit 6 stitches, then knit 6 stitches from cable needle
cm	centimetre(s)
cn	cable needle
CO	cast on
cont	continue
dec	decrease/decreases/decreasing
dpn	double pointed needle(s)
foll	follow/follows/following
g	gram
inc	increase/increases/increasing
k or K	knit
k1b	knit one stitch below
k2tog	knit 2 stitches together
k2tog tbl	knit 2 stitches together through back loops

kb1	knit into back of next stitch
kfb	knit into front and back of next stitch
kwise	knitwise
LH	left hand
lp(s)	loop(s)
m	metre(s)
M1	make one – a knitwise increase
M1 p-st	make one – a purlwise increase
MC	main color
mm	millimetre(s)
p or P	purl
patt(s)	pattern(s)
p2tog	purl 2 stitches together
p2tog tbl	purl 2 stitches together through back loops
psso	pass slipped stitch over – also known as skpo
pwise	purlwise
rem	remain/remaining
rep	repeat(s)
rev st st	reverse stocking stitch
RH	right hand
rnd(s)	round(s)
RS	right side
skpo	slip, knit, pass stitch over (also known as psso) – a one-stitch decrease
sk2p	slip 1, knit 2 together, pass slip stitch over the knit 2 together – a two-stitch decrease
sl	slip
sl1k	slip 1 knitwise
sl1p	slip 1 purlwise
sl st	slip stitch(es)
ssk	slip, slip, knit these 2 stiches together – a one-stitch decrease
sssk	slip, slip, slip, knit 3 stitches together
st(s)	stitch(es)
st st	stocking stitch
tbl	through back loop
tog	together
WS	wrong side
yb	yarn back – as if to knit
yd(s)	yard(s)
yf	yarn forward – as if to purl
yo	yarn over (also known as yon)
yrn	yarn around needle
yon	yarn over needle

Terminology

Sometimes understanding a knitting pattern can seem like battling with a foreign language. Whilst it may seem baffling at first, once you pick up a few key phrases you will be fluent!

Alt rows this is used when you have to work something on every alternate row, most usually shaping

At front edge the edge that meets in the centre, sometimes the edge with a buttonhole or button band

At side edge the edge you will sew to another piece of knitting, usually referred to when knitting a cardigan

At the same time used when you are shaping a garment and you need to do different shapings on different edges. For example, you may be decreasing for the armhole and at the same time decreasing for the neck

Cast off to fininsh off an edge and keep stitches from unraveling by lifting the first stitch over the second, the second over the third, and so on

Cast off in rib maintain the rib patterns as you cast off (knit the knit stitches; purl the purl stitches)

Cast on form a foundation row by making a specified number of loops on the knitting needle

Cont in patt/as set continue to work in the pattern that has been established in the preceding rows

Decrease reduce the number of stitches in a row (for example, knit 2 together; purl 2 together)

Increase add to the number of stitches in a row (for example, knit in front and back of stitch)

Integral edge a number of stitches worked in a contrast stitch or texture at the same time as the main knitting to give a 'seamless' finish (for example, buttonbands or edges of a throw)

Knit one stitch below (K1B) insert the right-hand needle into the next stitch but in the row below the stitch on the left-hand needle. Then knit the stitch as normal (see right)

Knitwise insert the needle into the stitch as if you were going to knit it

Make one with tip of needle, lift strand between last stitch worked and next stitch on left-hand needle, place strand on left-hand needle and knit into back of it to increase one stitch

On 4th and on every foll 6th row usually used for shaping: work three rows then work the decrease or increase (whichever is specified) on the fourth row. Work five more rows then decrease or increase as specified in the sixth row. You then continue to work five rows and increase or decrease on the sixth row until you have completed the required number of increases or decreases

Pick up and knit/purl knit or purl into the loops along an edge for the numbers of stitches stated

Place markers loop a piece of contrasting yarn or stitch marker onto the needle or ends of row

Purlwise insert the needle into stitch as if you were going to purl it

Rep from * repeat the instructions given after the *

Reverse shaping this usually appears in the pattern for a garment where one half, such as the right front, must mirror the other half, the left front

Selvedge edge/stitch the edge stitch which helps to make seaming easier

Slip stitch pass a stitch from the left-hand to the right-hand needle as if to purl without working it

Turn stop working at this point (ignore the stitches unworked on the left-hand needle), turn and work on these stitches as instructed

Work straight/even continue in specified pattern without increasing or decreasing

Work to last 2 sts work across the row until there are two stitches (or number stated) on the left-hand needle

Yarn over make a new stitch by placing the yarn over the right-hand needle (yfwd, yon, yrn)

Seaming

A beautiful piece of knitting can be ruined by poor finishing, so take ample time when making up a project. Alongside back stitch (see page 73), I almost exclusively use mattress stitch – an invisible seaming method – for joining seams. Unlike other hand-knit designers, I prefer not to use the yarn end from the piece when making up. Instead, I use a fresh length of yarn or thread. This is for the simple reason that it is easier to close the seam by gently pulling the thread from both ends. When pulled from just the one end, the strain can often lead to the yarn breaking.

Joining two selvedges

Thread a blunt-ended sewing needle with a length of yarn. With right sides up, lay the two pieces of knitting to be joined selvedge to selvedge. On the right-hand piece, from the front, take the needle under the first two horizontal bars that divide the stitches from the ones above. Take the needle across to the left-hand piece and then, from the front, take the needle under the equivalent two horizontal bars. Continue in this way, switching from the right-hand side to the left, picking up two bars each time, until the seam is completed. Stop at regular intervals of approximately 5cm to gently drawing up the thread to close the seam.

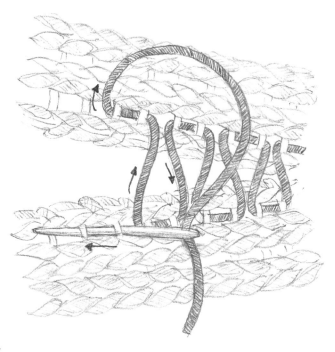

Joining a cast-off edge to a selvedge

Thread a blunt-ended sewing needle with a length of yarn. With right sides up, lay the two pieces of knitting to be joined cast-off edge to selvedge. On the cast-off edge, from the back to the front, take the needle through the centre of the first stitch. Next, take the needle under one or two horizontal bars (depending on whether or not the stitch is as wide as it is long) between the first and second stitches of the selvedge and then back through the centre of the same stitch on the cast-off edge. Continue in this way, switching from cast-off edge to selvedge, until the seam is completed.

Joining a rib seam with knit stitch edges

With right sides up, lay the two pieces of knitting to be joined selvedge to selvedge. On the right-hand piece, from the front, take the needle under the horizontal bar in the centre of the first knit stitch. Take the needle across to the left-hand piece and then, from the front, take the needle under the equivalent horizontal bar. Continue in this way, gently drawing up the thread, to form one complete knit stitch along the seam.

Joining a rib seam with purl stitch edges

Skip the purl stitch at the edge of each piece and join the seam at the centre of the first knit stitches, as for joining two knit stitch edges.

Joining a rib seam with knit and purl stitch edges

Skip the purl stitch at the edge of one piece of knitting and join the seam at the centre of the irst knit stitches, as for joining two knit stitch edges.

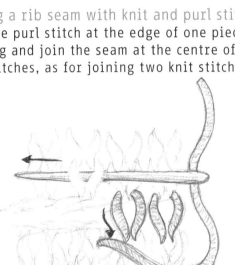

1

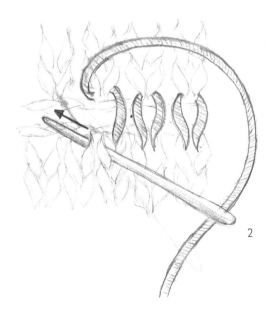

2

Joining two cast-off edges

1 Thread a blunt-ended sewing needle with a length of yarn. With right sides up, lay the two pieces of knitting to be joined with the cast-off edges butted together. On the lower piece, from the back to the front, take the needle through the centre of the first stitch just below the cast-off edge. Next, take the needle through the centre of the first stitch on the upper piece and out through the centre of the next stitch.

2 Next, take the needle through the centre of the first stitch on the lower piece again and out through the centre of the next stitch to the left. Continue in this way, switching from the lower piece to the upper piece, until the seam is completed.

Troubleshooting

So what do you do when things go wrong? Even the best of knitters occasionally drop a stitch or go astray from a pattern and have to unravel their work. If it happens to you, don't despair and don't panic. With a dropped stitch, keep the work as still as possible so as not to unravel the stitch further or ensure that it doesn't travel by securing it with a safety pin. And on unravelling mistakes, although it may be demoralising at the time to undo lots of rows, it is better to correct an error straightaway than continue regardless and regret it forever more!

Picking up a dropped stitch on a knit row

Work to the dropped stitch. Make sure the dropped stitch is sitting in front of the loose horizontal strand of the above row. Put the tip of a crochet hook into the loop of the dropped stitch from front to back and then, using the hook, catch the horizontal strand and pull it through the stitch. The strand has now become a stitch. Repeat as many times as necessary until the dropped stitch has been picked up through all the rows. Put the last stitch picked up onto the left-hand needle to be knitted.

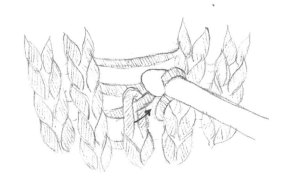

Picking up a dropped stitch on a purl row

Work to the dropped stitch. Make sure the dropped purl stitch is sitting behind the loose horizontal strand of the above row. Put the tip of a crochet hook into the loop of the dropped stitch from back to front and then, using the hook, catch the horizontal strand and pull it through the stitch. The strand has now become a stitch. Repeat as many times as necessary until all dropped stitch has been picked up through all the rows. Put the last stitch picked up onto the left-hand needle to be knitted.

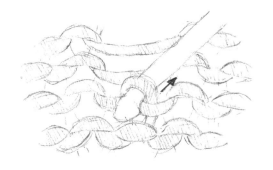

Unravelling stitch by stitch on a knit row

Put the tip of the left-hand needle into the front of the first stitch below the first stitch on the right-hand needle. Let the stitch drop off the right-hand needle and tug the yarn to pull the stitch free. Repeat this until you reach the mistake to be corrected.

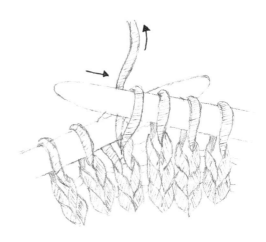

Unravelling stitch by stitch on a purl row

Put the tip of the left-hand needle into the front of the first stitch below the first stitch on the right-hand needle. Let the stitch drop off the right-hand needle and tug the yarn to pull the stitch free. Repeat this until you reach the mistake to be corrected.

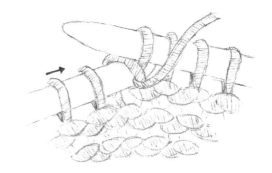

Unravelling several rows

Take the knitting off both needles and slowly and carefully pull out the yarn, unravelling the stitches, until you reach the row with the mistake. Holding the knitting in your left hand and the needle in your right, put the tip of the needle into the first stitch of the unravelled loops. Continue in this way until all the stitches are back on the needle.

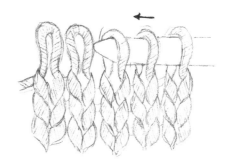

Understanding patterns

When it comes to understanding knitting patterns, there are many shared conventions and terminology. Though designers and yarn companies may use slight variations in their styles, the same information should always be given. Before purchasing yarn for any project, read through the pattern to ensure you understand exactly what is needed.

Size

For homewares and accessories, patterns usually come in a single size. For garments, however, I like to give a choice of sizes ranging from extra small to extra large. For the sweater and cardigan on pages 134–41 I have given the actual measurements of the finished knitted piece as well as the recommended chest measurement each size is designed to fit. Depending on the intended fit of a garment – whether it is loose or tight fitting – these two measurements will not necessarily be the same.

Materials

The pattern specifies what type of yarn is needed for the project, along with the total number of balls. When the pattern is for a garment that comes in different sizes, the number of balls needed for each size will be stated. Also given in the materials list will be the size of knitting needles required, which could be one or more pairs, as well as any closures, such as buttons and zips, or trims.

Tension

The tension, or stitch gauge, indicates how many stitches and rows you must have to a certain measurement, usually 10cm square. Your tension needs to be correct to achieve the exact dimensions given in a pattern (see pages 36–7 for more on this). Achieving an exact tension is less critical for a throw or a cushion than for a garment. A difference in tension when knitting a garment will not only affect the finishied dimensions but will also alter on the amount of yarn needed to complete the project.

Pattern instructions

The pattern works through the individual elements of the project, giving all the necessary instructions for each part. Every pattern begins with the size of needles and shade of yarn used (if more than one colour is used), and number of stitches cast on. The pattern will continue to outline, row by row, the stitch pattern to follow and indicate when any shaping or other details, such as buttonholes, should be worked. It can take a while to become familiar with the language of knitting patterns, so on pages 38 and 39 I have listed the most commonly used abbreviations and added a glossary of phrases.

When following any pattern, you need to be aware of the different usage of round brackets ( ) and square brackets [ ]. Round brackets ( ) indicate the different measurements or stitches given for multiple sizes. The sizes given for the sweater on pages 134–37 are extra-small, small, medium, large and extra-large. If you choose to knit the medium size, then you need to follow the third size given in the pattern instructions. So where the instructions state: *Using 3.25mm needles, cast on 97 (103: 109: 115: 119) sts* to knit the medium size you must cast on 109 stitches, the third number listed. The first size is always shown outside the brackets and the remaining sizes within them. Likewise, brackets are used for specific measurements within a pattern of different sizes. So where the instructions state: *Cont in stocking stitch until work measures 37 (38: 39: 40: 41)cm* to knit the medium size, again, you must follow the third measurement listed which is 39cm.

Do also be aware that many knitting patterns use square brackets or parentheses [ ]. These square brackets have nothing to do with sizing but relate to repeating instructions (see page 38).

Making up or finishing

This tells you how to sew up your completed pieces in order to get the best finish.

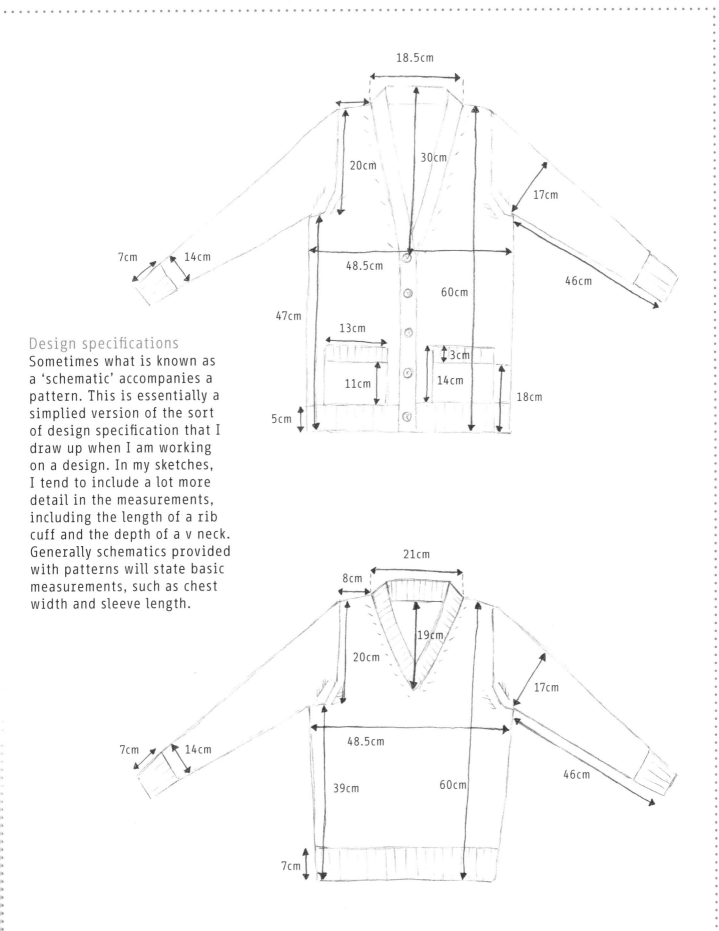

18.5cm

20cm

30cm

17cm

7cm   14cm

48.5cm

60cm

46cm

47cm

13cm

3cm

11cm

14cm

5cm

18cm

Design specifications

Sometimes what is known as a 'schematic' accompanies a pattern. This is essentially a simplied version of the sort of design specification that I draw up when I am working on a design. In my sketches, I tend to include a lot more detail in the measurements, including the length of a rib cuff and the depth of a v neck. Generally schematics provided with patterns will state basic measurements, such as chest width and sleeve length.

21cm

8cm

19cm

20cm

17cm

7cm   14cm

48.5cm

39cm   60cm

46cm

7cm

Reading charts

Instead of being written out row by row using the abbreviations and terms on pages 44–5, a stitch pattern can be represented as a chart on graph paper. Each square of the chart represents one stitch, and each line of squares represents one row of knitting. Different stitches are denoted by either a colour or a symbol, specified in a key.

With both types chart, the right side rows (or odd numbered knit rows) are read from right to left, while the wrong side rows (or even numbered purl rows) are read from left to right. The rows of the chart are read from the bottom to the top.

Likewise, colourwork instructions can either be written out in full within the pattern or represented as a chart. The various shades of yarn that make up the colourwork motif are represented either as a shaded colour (right) or as a symbol (far right).

Key

	C Brown
	A Light Grey
	B Dark Grey
	C Brown
	A Light Grey
	B Dark Grey

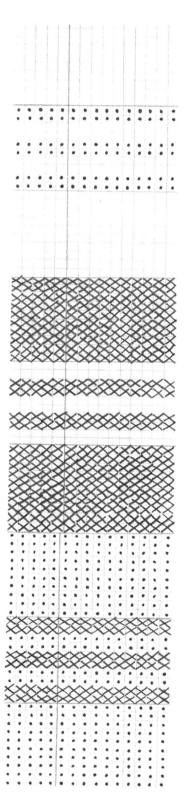

Aftercare

After investing so much time creating a hand knit, great care should be taken in the laundering. How frequent a garment needs washing depends on how it is worn or used. Many of the projects in this book may not need laundering on a regular basis. If it does, the yarn you use must be able to withstand this, but this does not necessarily mean that all yarns must be machine washable. Look at the labels: those on most commercial yarns have instructions for washing or dry cleaning, drying and pressing. So, for a project knitted in a single yarn, a quick look at the label will tell you how to care for it. If you wish to work with several yarns in one project, the aftercare requires a little more thought. If one label states dry clean only, then dry clean the garment.

Washing

If in doubt about whether or not your knitting is washable, then make a little swatch of the yarns. Wash this to see if the fabric is affected by being immersed in water or not, watching for shrinkage and stretching. If satisfied with the results, go ahead and wash the knitting by hand in lukewarm water. Never use hot water, as this will 'felt' your fabric, and you will not be able to return it to its pre-washed state. In particular, wool tends to react to major changes in temperature.

When washing any knitted item, handle it carefully. There should be enough water to cover the garment completely and the soap should be thoroughly dissolved before immersing it. If you need to sterilise a badly soiled or stained garment, then use a proprietary brand of steriliser for this purpose.

As a precaution, test wash any trims you use before you make up the garment with them. Nothing is more infuriating than to spoil an entire garment because the trim colours run in the wash. Natural fibres such as wool, cotton and silk are usually better washed by hand, and in pure soap, than in a machine. Should you decide to wash any knitted garment in a machine, place it inside a pillowslip as an extra precaution. Soap flakes are kinder to sensitive skins than most detergents, provided all traces of the soap are removed in the rinsing process.

Rinsing

Squeeze out any excess water, never wring it out. Rinse thoroughly, until every trace of soap is removed; any left will mat the fibres and may irritate the skin. Use at least two changes of water or continue until the water is clear and without soap bubbles. Keep the rinsing water the same temperature as the washing water.

Spinning

Garments can be rinsed on a short rinse and spin as part of the normal washing machine programme for delicate fabrics. Again, as an extra precaution, place the item to be spun inside a pillowslip.

Drying

Squeeze the garment between towels or fold in a towel and gently spin. Do not hang wet knitting up to dry, as the weight of the water will stretch it out of shape. To dry, lay the knitting out flat on top of a towel, which will absorb some of the moisture. Ease the garment into shape. Dry away from direct heat and leave flat until completely dry.

Pressing

When the garment is dry, ease it into shape. Check the yarn label before pressing your knitting as most fibres only require a little steam, and the iron should be applied gently. Alternatively, press with a damp cloth between the garment and the iron.

Removing stains

Stains are a fact of life. The best solution with any stain is to remove the garment while the stain is still wet and soak it thoroughly in cold, never hot, water. Failing that, use a proprietary stain remover.

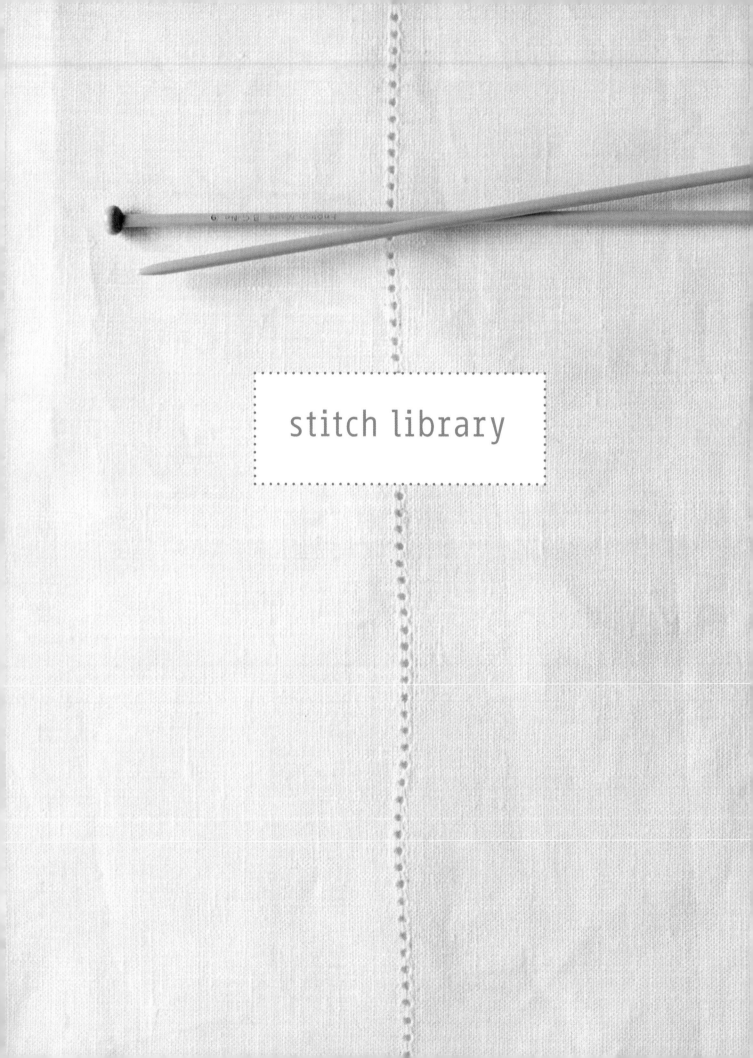

stitch library

basic stitches

Worked over any number of stitches

Knit every row.

Garter Stitch

- the first stitch to master
- creates a firm, neat fabric
- rows look like little 'waves'
- when counting rows, one row of 'waves' is two rows of knitting

Worked over any number of stitches

Row 1 (RS) Knit.
Row 2 Purl.
Rep these 2 rows.

Stocking Stitch

- creates a basic smooth fabric, with one side of tiny 'V's, most often called the right side
- the 'V's are easy to count when checking tension

Reverse Stocking Stitch

- creates a good alternative texture
- looks similar to garter stitch but makes a lighter fabric

Worked over any number of stitches

Row 1 (RS) Purl.
Row 2 Knit.
Rep these 2 rows.

Twisted Stocking Stitch

- this stitch creates a simple surface texture
- when I started to knit, I was working twisted stocking stitch by mistake

Worked over any number of stitches

Row 1 (RS) Knit into back of every stitch.
Row 2 Purl.
Rep these 2 rows.

rib stitches

Worked over an even number of stitches

* K1, p1, rep from *
to end.
Rep this row.

Worked over an odd number of stitches

Row 1 K1, * P1, K1,
rep from * to end.
Row 2 P1, * K1, P1,
rep from * to end.
Rep these 2 rows.

Worked over a multiple of 4 sts

* K2, p2, rep from *
to end.
Rep this row.

Worked over a multiple of 4 sts plus 2 sts

Row 1 K2, * p2, k2, rep
from * to end.
Row 2 P2, * k2, p2, rep
from * to end.
Rep these 2 rows.

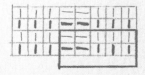

K1, P1 Rib

- a classic stitch to knit
- usually the beginning stitch
for sweaters and cardigans
- gives elasticity to cuffs, welts
and collars

K2, P2 Rib

- a variation on basic rib;
probably the most popular
- great for close-fitting
garments and
'New Yorker'
style hats

K3, P2 Rib

- one of my favourite rib set ups
- I prefer to use odd-number ribs, especially for menswear

Worked over a multiple of 5 sts plus 3 sts

Row 1 * K3, p2, rep from * to last 3 sts, k3.
Row 2 P3, * K2, p3, rep from * to end.
Rep these 2 rows.

Worked over a multiple of 5 sts plus 2 sts

Row 1 * P2, k3, rep from * to last 2 sts, p2.
Row 2 * K2, p3, rep from * to last 2 sts, k2.
Rep these 2 rows.

Slip Stitch Rib

- creates an interesting linen-like surface
- requires concentration in taking the yarn forward and back

Worked over a multiple of 2 sts plus 1 st

Row 1 (WS) Purl.
Row 2 K1, * yf, sl 1 purlwise, yb, k1, rep from * to end.
Rep these 2 rows.

texture stitches

Worked over any
number of stitches

Rows 1 (RS), 3 (RS)
and 4 (WS) Knit.
Row 2 Purl.
Rep these 4 rows.

Purl Bar Stitch

- an easy and effective
way to lift a plain garment or
project with simple texture rows
- creates what is called
a 'semi-plain'
textile

Worked over a multiple
of 4 sts plus 3 sts

Row 1 (RS) K1, * p1,
k3, rep from * to last
2 sts, p1, k1.
Row 2 Purl.
Row 3 K3, p1, rep from
* to last 3 sts, k3.
Row 4 Purl.
Rep these 4 rows.

Dot Stitch

- derives its inspiration from
woven fabric
- creates a discreet 'dobby'
look pattern

Mock Rib Stitch

- a useful replacement for rib that doesn't pull in the fabric
- the reverse creates an interesting basket weave effect

Worked over a multiple of 2 sts plus 1 st

Row 1 (RS) K1, * p1, k1, rep from * to end.
Row 2 P1, * keeping yarn at front of work sl 1 purlwise, p1, rep from * to end.
Rep these 2 rows.

Uneven Rib Stitch

- a 'staggered' rib stitch that has pronounced lines of single knit stitches
- this stitch gives the illusion of greater depth than other ribs

Worked over a multiple of 4 sts plus 3 sts

K2, p2, rep from * to last 3 sts, k2, p1.
Rep this row.

texture
stitches

Worked over a multiple of 2 sts plus 1 st

K1, * p1, k1; rep from * to end.
Rep this row.

Moss Stitch

– *reversible stitch*
– *firm texture*
– *suitable for both fine and fat yarns*

Worked over a multiple of 2 sts plus 1 st

Row 1 (WS) P1, * KB1, p1; rep from * to end.
Row 2 Knit.
Row 3 * KB1, p1; rep from * to last st, KB1.
Row 4 Knit.
Rep these 4 rows.

See abbreviations on page 38 for KB1

Double Rice Stitch

– *beautiful stitch to work in fine cotton*

Herringbone Stitch

- *makes a natural decorative edge*
- *perfect stitch for scarves and sweaters*

Worked over a multiple of 7 sts plus 1 st

Row 1 (WS) Purl.
Row 2 * K2tog, k2, K1B Back then knit st above, k2; rep from * to last st, k1.
Row 3 Purl.
Row 4 K3, K1B Back then knit st above, k2, k2tog, * k2, K1B Back then knit st above, k2, k2tog; rep from * to end.
Rep these 4 rows.

See illustration on page 39 for K1B

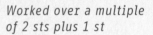

Worked over a multiple of 2 sts plus 1 st

Row 1 (RS) K1, * yf, sl1 purlwise, yb, k1; rep from * to end.
Row 2 P2, * yb, sl1 purlwise, yf, p1; rep from * to last st, p1.
Rep these 2 rows.

Tweed Stitch

- *reversible stitch*
- *firm fabric for homewares projects*
- *go up a size needle for a more fluid fabric*

cable stitches

See abbreviations on page 38 for cable stitches

Worked over a panel of 4 sts on reverse stocking stitch

Row 1 (RS) Knit.
Row 2 Purl.
Row 3 C4B.
Row 4 Purl.
Rep these 4 rows.
The cable twists to the right.
To work the cable to the left, in row 3 instead of C4B, work C4F where the cable needle is held at the front of work.

Worked over a panel of 8 sts on reverse stocking stitch

Row 1 (RS) Knit.
Row 2 Purl.
Rows 3 and 4 Rep rows 1 and 2.
Row 5 C8B.
Row 6 Purl.
Rows 7–10 Rep rows 1 and 2 twice more.
Rep these 10 rows.
The cable twists to the right.
To work the cable to the left, in row 5 instead of C8B, work C8F where the cable needle is held at the front of the work.

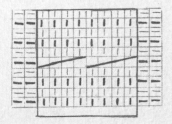

4-Stitch Cable

- the simplest of all the cables
- use in little neat rows
- reminiscent of the traditional cricket sweaters

8-Stitch Cable

- although simple to do, this cabling looks very clever!
- it is easy to twist cables to either the right or the left

Worked over a panel of 12 sts on reverse stocking stitch

Row 1 (RS): Knit.
Row 2: Purl.
Row 3: C12B.
Row 4: Purl.
Rows 5–16: Rep rows 1 and 2 six times more.
Rep these 16 rows.

Large Cable

- oversized cables adds an extra dynamic
- a sculptural stitch perfect for homewares, garments, and accessories

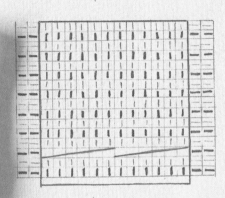

Plait

- twisting stitches to both the front and the back sounds more complex than it really is
- plaited cables can travel all over knitting

Worked over a panel of 12 sts on reverse stocking stitch

Row 1 (RS): Knit.
Row 2: Purl.
Row 3: C8F, k4.
Row 4: Purl.
Rows 5–8: Rep rows 1 and 2 twice more.
Row 9: K4, C8B.
Row 10: Purl.
Rows 11–12: Rep rows 1 and 2.
Rep these 12 rows.

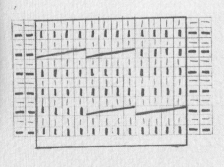

cable stitches   **59**

stripe sequences

*Worked over 39 rows
in stocking stitch*

A (grey) 4 rows
B (ecru) 1 row
C (blue) 9 rows
B (ecru) 2 rows
D (fawn) 2 rows
B (ecru) 1 row
D (chocolate) 4 rows
B (ecru) 2 rows
A (grey) 6 rows
B (ecru) 3 rows
D (fawn) 5 rows

**Five-Colour
Stripe**

*- shade of blue
with earthy browns
always create
a popular,
classic colourway*

*Worked over 39 rows
in stocking stitch*

A (fawn) 6 rows
B and C (chocolate
and blue) 1 row
A (fawn) 5 rows
C (blue) 1 row
A (fawn) 5 rows
B and C (chocolate
and blue) 1 row
A (fawn) 5 rows
B and C (chocolate
and blue) 1 row
A (fawn) 5 rows
B and C (chocolate
and blue) 1 row
A (fawn) 5 rows
B and C (chocolate
and blue) 1 row
A (fawn) 4 rows

**Three-Colour
Stripe**

*- this 'broken' stripe variation
gives vibrancy to a simple
three-colour layout*

Five-Colour Stripe

*‒ ‒ I prefer an odd number
of stripe rows, especially
single row stripes
‒ single rows are time consuming,
joining in ends, but effective*

*Worked over 36 rows
in stocking stitch*

A (grey) 5 rows
B (lime) 2 rows
C (ecru) 2 rows
B (lime) 2 rows
D (fawn) 1 row
E (chocolate) 1 row
D (fawn) 1 row
E (chocolate) 1 row
D (fawn) 1 row
E (chocolate) 1 row
D (fawn) 1 row
E (chocolate) 1 row
D (fawn) 1 row
E (chocolate) 1 row
D (fawn) 1 row
E (chocolate) 1 row
D (fawn) 1 row
E (chocolate) 1 row
D (fawn) 1 row
E (chocolate) 1 row
D (fawn) 1 row
B (lime) 2 rows
C (ecru) 2 rows
B (lime) 1 row
A (grey) 3 rows

Multi-Colour Stripe

*‒ neutral tones work
with strong brights
‒ zesty lime is one
of my favourite
accent colours*

*Worked over 39 rows
in stocking stitch*

A (fawn) 8 rows
B (ecru) 3 rows
C (chocolate) 2 rows
B (ecru) 2 rows
D (lime) 8 rows
B (ecru) 1 row
E (grey) 3 rows
B (ecru) 2 rows
C (chocolate) 3 rows
B (ecru) 1 row
A (fawn) 2 rows
B (ecru) 1 row
D (lime) 3 rows

project
workshops

1 Muffler

A simple yet chic little muffler knitted in the most basic stitch of all — garter stitch — which means it's the perfect· first-time project. Make this scarf in a luxurious royal alpaca yarn to create a neat accessory from a refined fabric. Alternatively, experiment with other fibres, such as a hand-dyed silk, to create a pronounced textural effect and an altogether more artisan textile.

Skill level...

◼◻◻◻
BEGINNER

In this project you will learn...

Gauging whether there is sufficient yarn to complete a row; weaving in yarn ends for a neat finish

Stitches used...

Garter stitch

Size
Approximately 14cm wide by 96cm long, depending on your tension

Materials
2 x 100g skeins fine alpaca yarn, such as
   Blue Sky Alpacas Royal **2** FINE
or
2 x 40g skeins fine silk yarn, such as
   Alchemy Yarns Silken Straw **2** FINE
Pair of 3mm knitting needles
Large blunt-ended sewing needle

Tension
28 stitches and 54 rows to 10cm over garter stitch using 3mm needles

To make the Muffler
Cast on 40 sts and work 96cm in garter stitch –
knit every row.
Cast off loosely.

To finish
Weave in any loose yarn ends. *See Masterclass,
below right.*
Lay the work out flat and gently steam the
finished piece.

Masterclass

Gauging whether there is sufficient yarn to complete a row
It is best not to run out of yarn in the middle
of a row. If you are almost at the end of a ball
of yarn and you are unsure whether you can
complete the next row, lay your work flat and
fold the remaining yarn back and forth over
the knitting. If you have at least four times
the width of your knitted piece, you will have
sufficient yarn to work a row of basic stitches,
such as garter or stocking stitch. Cables, ribs
and texture stitches take more yarn.

Weaving in yarn ends for a neat finish
Whenever possible, join new balls of yarn
at the beginning or end of a row. Once the
project is finished, weave the loose yarn ends
into either the fabric or the seams. As this
garter stitch muffler is reversible, there is
no 'wrong side' to the project in which to
hide the yarn ends so simply choose one side
to work the ends into. Looking at the garter
stitch fabric from one side, stretch it a little
so that the rows spread apart – you will see
one row of knitted 'V's alternated with one
row of purl bumps. Using a large blunt-ended
needle threaded with the yarn end, weave
it in along the row of recessed knitted 'V's,
mimicking the path of the yarn in that row to
effectively camouflage it within the fabric.

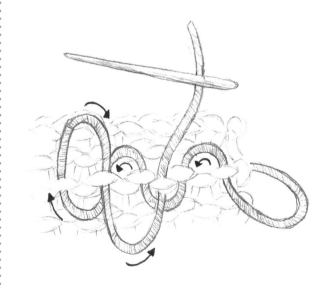

Dishcloth

A small knitted project to practise a basic texture stitch, which can then be put to good use as a practical, thrifty and environmentally friendly dishcloth. Knitted in unbleached natural cotton, this cloth is worked in moss stitch, which uses both knit and purl stitches alternately to create a bumpy textured, double-faced fabric. The instructions given below include a handy technique of working knit stitches at the end of every row to give a neat finish.

Skill level...

BEGINNER

In this project you will learn...

Achieving a neat selvedge by working a knit stitch at the end of each row; reusing yarn by rewinding

Stitches used...

Moss stitch; garter stitch

Size
Approximately 21cm wide by 26cm high

Materials
1 x 100g ball light-weight DK cotton yarn, such as
  Jarol King Dishcloth Cotton **3** LIGHT
  – 100g of yarn makes two cloths
Pair of 4.5mm knitting needles
Large blunt-ended sewing needle

Tension
19 stitches and 30 rows to 10cm square over moss stitch using 4.5mm needles

To make the Dishcloth
Cast on 39 sts and work 4 rows in garter stitch – knit every row.
Cont in moss stitch as folls:
Next row * K1, p1, rep from * to last st, k1.
Rep last row until work measures 24.5cm from cast-on edge.
Work 4 rows in garter stitch. Cast off.

To finish
Weave in any loose yarn ends. *See Masterclass, page 67.*
Lay the work out flat and gently steam.

Masterclass

Using an alternative stitch texture
I have used moss stitch for my dishcloth as its bumpy surface is perfect for tackling dirty crockery. Any stitch with a rough texture, such as garter stitch or purl bar stitch work equally well. *See Stitch Library, pages 50 and 54.*

Reusing yarn
Maybe you have kept a favourite sweater, much loved and worn, simply because you remember the time it took to make or the cost of the yarn. Well, provided it is not too felted, put it to good use once more. Remove any dirt – it will be washed later – unpick the seams, find the cast-off edge and unravel each piece of knitting in turn. The yarn will be wavy, but persist. Make a skein using either a commercially available wool winder or winding the yarn around the back of a chair. Tie the skein in several places to stop it becoming tangled. Now wash the yarn. Once dry it will be straight and ready to re-use.

3 Fold-over Cushion

A stylish cushion created from one long
piece of knitting, which is simply folded,
seamed and stuffed with a feather pad.
The open edge of the cover then folds over
to the front, enclosing the cushion pad.
Make this project in a variety of colours
or textures. Here, I have paired pure silk
with a mohair blend yarn, both in stocking
stitch. Alternatively, work the covers in a
different stitch; experiment with any of
the basic or texture stitches given in the
Stitch Library on pages 50–51 and 54–7.

Skill level...

■□□□

BEGINNER

In this project you will learn...

Creating a neat seam using back stitch

Stitches used...

Stocking stitch

Size
To fit a 40cm square cushion pad
Actual size of knitted piece:
140cm long by 40cm wide

Materials
4 x 50g balls light-weight DK silk yarn, such as
   Rowan Pure Silk DK **3** LIGHT
or
8 x 25g balls light-weight mohair DK yarn, such as
   Rowan Kid Silk Aura **3** LIGHT
Pair each of 3.75mm and 4mm knitting needles
Large blunt-ended sewing needle
40cm x 40cm feather cushion pad

Tension
22 stitches and 30 rows to 10cm square over stocking
stitch using 4mm needles

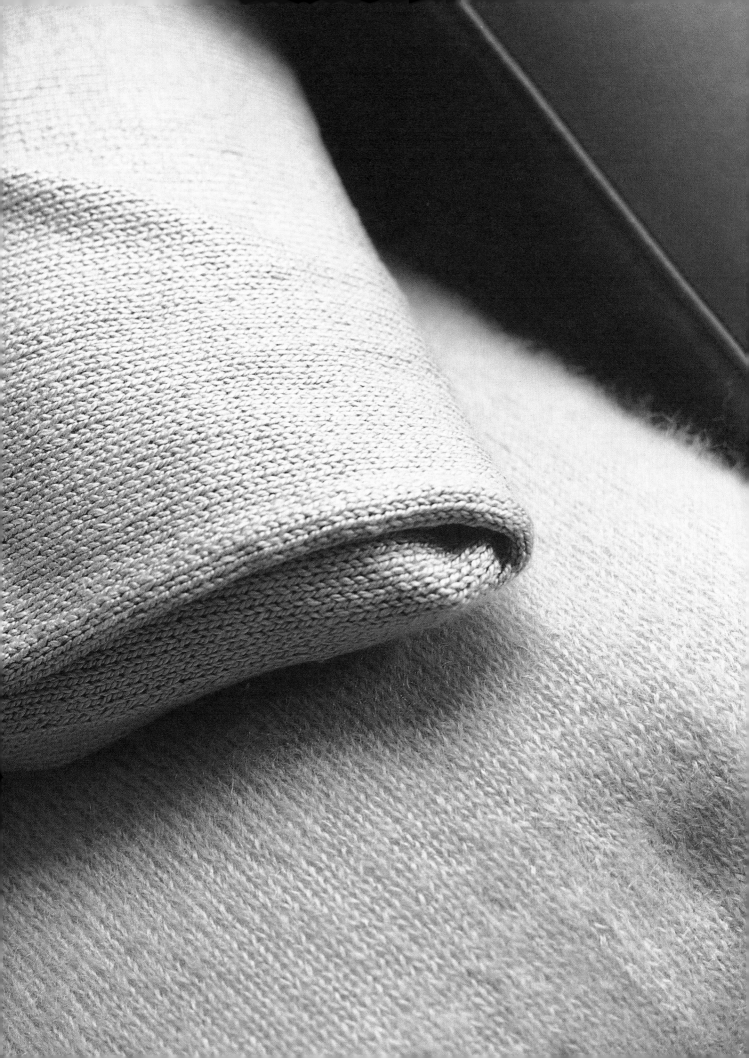

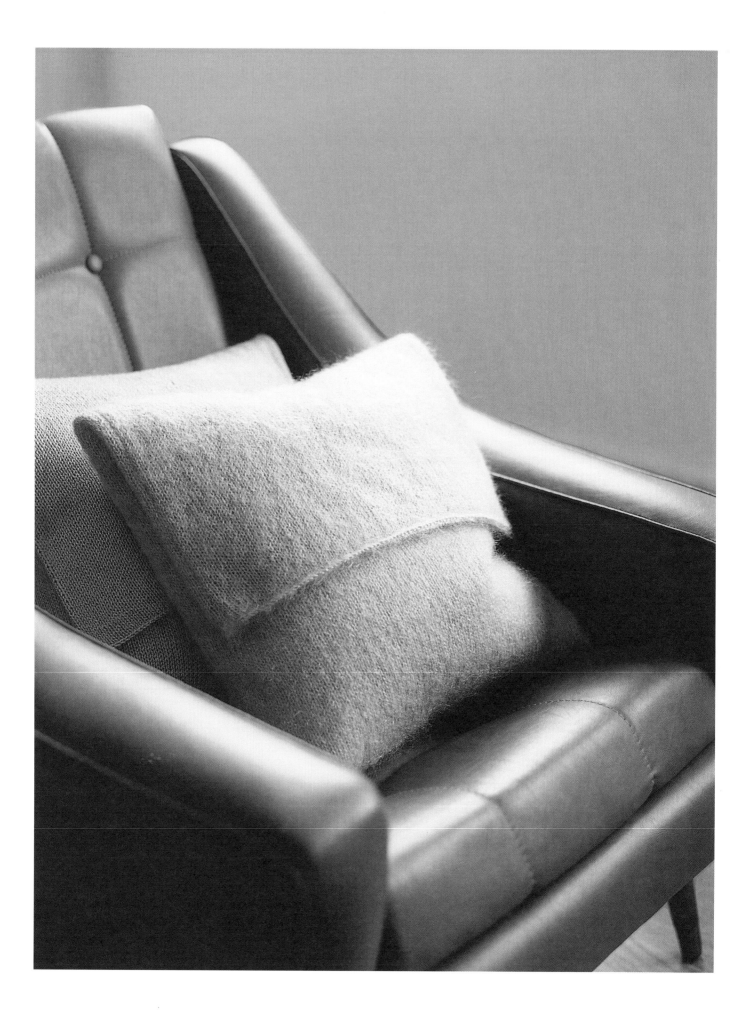

To make the Fold-over Cushion

Using 3.75mm needles, cast on 88 sts and beg with a knit row work 6 rows in stocking stitch – knit one row and purl one row alternately.
Change to 4mm needles and cont in stocking stitch until work measures 138cm from cast-on edge, ending with RS facing for next row.
Change to 3.75mm needles and work 6 rows in stocking stitch.
Cast off.

To finish

Weave in any loose yarn ends. *See Masterclass, page 67.*
Lay the work out flat and gently steam the finished piece on the reverse.
With RS together, fold work in half across width and join both side seams using back stitch. *See Masterclass, below right.*
Turn cushion cover right side out.
Place cushion pad inside cover and fold over excess fabric to front to make a flap.

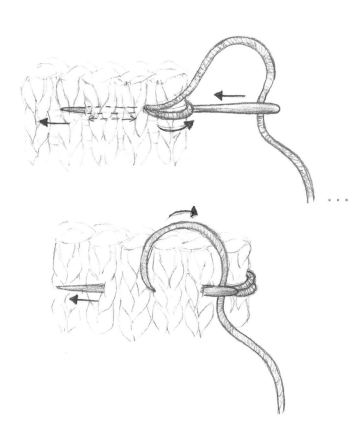

Masterclass

Achieving a neat cast-off edge

Achieving a neat, even tension across a cast-off row can be tricky. You may find that your cast-off edge is a little tighter than the rest of your knitted fabric. This can be easily remedied by using needles that are one size larger than asked for in the pattern, which will loosen the stitches and give the edge greater elasticity.

For this cushion I have cast on and cast off with a size smaller needle to deliberately create a firmer edge. Furthermore, I have cast off the stitches on a knit row so that the cast-off edge lies flat on the right side of the work and is clearly visible, giving the edge a slight roll. If you were to finish with a purlwise cast-off row, this edge would not be so visible on the right side.

Seaming using backstitch

Backstitch is the simplest and quickest way of joining together pieces of knitting. As it is worked on the wrong side, backstitch seams are not ideal when you need to match up specific stitches or patterns. However, for plain stocking stitch, backstitch creates a good strong seam that is not too bulky.

Place the two pieces to be joined right sides together. Before you begin to sew, pin these pieces evenly along the length of the seam.

Thread a blunt-ended sewing needle with a length of yarn. Starting at the right-hand side, bring the needle through both layers of knitting from the back to the front approximately one stitch in from the edge. Then either take the needle back through the knitted fabric approximately one stitch back from where it first came out or take the needle around the end of the piece. Next bring the needle back through to the front approximately one stitch in front of where you started. Pull up the yarn to tighten the stitch.

Continue along the seam, taking the needle backwards and then fowards through both layers of knitted fabric until you have completed the seam. Fasten off.

4 Notebook

This very simple notebook cover is worked in beginner's stocking stitch with a contrast reverse stocking stitch spine and neat selvedge edge. Filled with a selection of textural handmade papers, the notebook is sewn along the spine to secure the pages. As additional decoration, the book can be finished with a contrast thread – leather, string or waxed cotton – and either tied in a bow or fastened around a button.

Skill level...

◖■□□▭
BEGINNER

In this project you will learn...

Adapting a pattern for a different yarn weight

Stitches used...

Stocking stitch; reverse stocking stitch

Size
Finished size of notebook once made up: approximately 14cm high by 10.5cm wide and 2cm deep
Actual size of knitted piece: 14cm high by 23cm wide

Materials
1 x 25g ball super fine cotton or silk yarn, such as Habu Cotton Gima or Alchemy Yarns Silken Straw
[1] SUPER FINE
Pair of 2.75mm knitting needles
or
1 x 25g ball fine silk yarn, such as Habu Silk Gima
[2] FINE
Pair of 3.25mm knitting needles

Handmade paper
Hole punch
Large blunt-ended sewing needle
Leather, string or waxed cotton (optional)
Button (optional)

Tension
The tension of the knitted piece will vary according to your chosen yarn. For the yarns used here, the tensions are as follows:
Super fine yarn: 36 stitches and 48 rows to 10cm square over stocking stitch using 2.75mm needles
Fine yarn: 26 stitches and 36 rows to 10cm square over stocking stitch using 3.25mm needles

Masterclass

Adapting a pattern for a different yarn weight

You can use any other type of yarn to knit these notebook covers; just remember to match the size of the knitting needles you use to your choice of yarn. Knit a tension sample and adjust the number of stitches cast on in order to make your knitted piece the size required.

This is where a calculator comes in handy. For example, to work out how many stitches you need to cast on to achieve a knitted piece with a width of 23cm if you used a medium-weight yarn with a tension of 22 stitches to 10cm square, divide 22 by 10 to get the number of stitches per 1cm – 2.2. Now multiply that number by 23 in order to get the amount of stitches needed to cast on to achieve the desired width of 23cm – 50.6. I then round that number up to the nearest whole number, so that makes 51 stitches for a knitted piece that is approximately 23cm wide.

To make the Notebook cover using superfine yarn

Using 2.75mm needles, cast on 87 sts and work as folls:
Row 1 (RS) P1, k1, p1, k1, p1, k34, p9, k34, p1, k1, p1, k1, p1.
Row 2 K1, p1, k1, p1, k1, p34, k9, p34, k1, p1, k1, p1, k1.
Rep these 2 rows until work measures 14cm ending with RS facing for next row.
Cast off.

To make the Notebook cover using fine yarn

Using 3.25mm needles, cast on 62 sts and work as folls:
Row 1 (RS) P1, k1, p1, k25, p6, k25, p1, k1, p1.
Row 2 K1, p1, k1, p25, k6, p25, k1, p1, k1.
Rep these 2 rows until work measures 14cm ending with RS facing for next row.
Cast off.

To finish

Weave in any loose yarn ends. *See Masterclass, page 67.*
Lay the work out flat and gently steam the finished piece.

To make the book pages

Cut or tear selected paper or papers to size for the leaves of the notebook.

Alternatively, use brown wrapping or parcel paper or any other fine-weight paper folded in half to make the notebook pages.

Using a hole punch, make three evenly spaced holes along the spine edge of the gathered leaves. Slot the leaves into the knitted book jacket, leaving the neat folded edge as the visible finished edge.

To sew in the book pages

Using either the same yarn as the cover or a contrast thread, such as string, double over the thread to create a loop at one end.

Thread a blunt-ended sewing needle with the doubled-over thread and knot at the free end. Pass the needle and thread through the centre hole [1] and secure by passing the needle through the loop and pulling up tight.

Next, pass the needle through the hole above [2] from front to back, then over the spine [3] and back down into the front of hole [2].

Then take the thread up along the back of the book, round the top end of the book's spine [4] to the front and again pass it through the hole [2] from front to back.

Next, take the thread along the back of the book's spine and up through the centre hole [1] from back to front

Repeat these steps for the other end of the book. Secure with a knot.

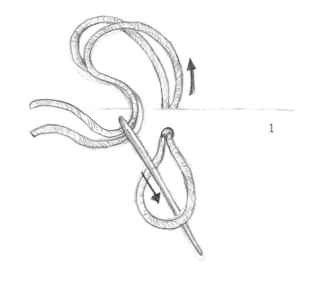

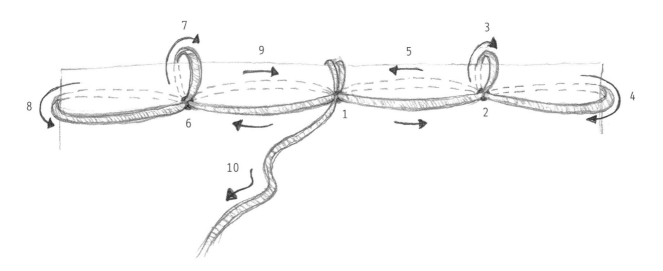

5 Shopper

This elegant bag is made up of nothing more than one long piece of knitting worked in chunky yarn and in a firm double-sided stitch. The knitted strip is then simply folded, stitched and finished with robust cotton webbing handles to create a useful holdall.

Skill level...

■◧■□▭
EASY

In this project you will learn...

Bringing yarn forward, slipping stitch purlwise and then taking yarn back to create tweed stitch; sewing on tape and taping a seam

Stitches used...

Tweed stitch

Size
Finished size of shopper once made up:
approx 42cm high by 38cm wide and 10cm deep
Actual size of knitted piece:
approx 104cm high by 39.5cm wide

Materials
9 x 50g balls super bulky wool yarn, such as
   Debbie Bliss Como (6) SUPER BULKY
Pair of 10mm knitting needles
Large blunt-ended sewing needle
3m cotton tape, 3.8cm wide, for handles
Strong sewing thread and needle

Tension
10 stitches and 15 rows to 10cm square over stocking stitch using 10mm needles

Notes
The tension is over stocking stitch as counting rows of tweed stitch is tricky. If the stocking stitch tension is correct, the tweed stitch tension will be correct.

To make the Shopper
worked in one piece

Cast on 53 sts and work in tweed stitch as folls:
Row 1 (RS) K1, * yf, sl1p, yb, k1; rep from *
to end.
Row 2 P2, * yb, sl1p, yf, p1; rep from * to last
stitch, p1.
Rep these 2 rows until work measures 104cm from
cast-on edge, ending with RS facing for next row.
Cast off tightly in k1, p1 rib to make a firm edge.

To finish

Weave in any loose yarn ends. *See Masterclass,
page 67.*
Lay the work out flat and gently steam the
finished piece on the reverse.
With RS together, fold work in half across length
and join both side seams using back stitch. *See
Masterclass, page 73.*
Fold top edge over to inside approximately 5cm
and stitch down.
To form the bag's base and gusset, with WS
out, take the tips of the sewn corners and
fold inwards to form a box shape (rather like
wrapping the edges of a parcel).
Stitch the folded corners down to the base of
the bag. Turn RS out (with the bigger stitch to
the front.)
Cut the cotton tape in half and attach to the bag
as folls:
Take one of the pieces and find the centre (that is
the centre of the handle).
Take each side in turn and pin along the length
of the bag, approximately 13cm apart, taking to
bottom of gusset and securing at base.
Stitch cotton tape into position using strong
sewing thread.
Repeat for other side of handle. Secure tape at
the bottom, overlapping the tape from other side,
and turning the end under.

Masterclass

Adding cotton tape handles
The wide cotton twill tape applied to this
shopper not only provides the bag with robust
handles but is also an integral design feature.
The tape is simply attached using small whip
stitches – diagonally slanted stitches – that
are evenly spaced along the length of tape.

Taping a seam
A narrow cotton twill tape or seam binding
can be used along the seams of any knitted
piece to prevent them from stretching. This
is particularly beneficial for areas such as
shoulders, which can sometimes sag and lose
their shape, as the tape stabilises the seam.
Likewise, taping a seam can also help to ease
in a shoulder that is too wide.

Cut a piece of tape the length of the desired
shoulder width and whip stitch the tape on
either side along the shoulder seam, easing in
the fullness as desired.

This method of taping a seam is also very
useful for covering unsightly joins along neck
edges and collars, where a bulky seam may
rub against the skin (see the sweater on page
135 and the cardigan on page 138). I tape the
neck seam of any babies' garments in order to
protect their more delicate skin.

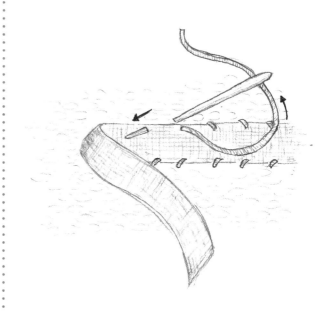

Stripe Cushion

A simple square cushion cover worked in the perennially popular stocking stitch using a palette of complementary earthy shades, plus a shot of lime, in this five-colour stripe. The back button fastening lends added decorative detail – and it is the perfect place to start practising how to work a buttonhole.

Skill level...

EASY

In this project you will learn...

Working in stripes; making a buttonhole

Stitches used...

Stocking stitch

Size
Finished size of cushion once made up:
approximately 40cm square
Actual size of knitted piece:
40cm wide by 80cm high

Materials
Light-weight DK yarn, such as Rowan Lenpur
Linen **3** LIGHT
    A 1 x 50g ball in dark grey
    B 2 x 50g balls in off white
    C 1 x 50g ball in dark brown
    D 1 x 50g ball in taupe
    E 1 x 50g ball in lime green
Pair each of 3.25mm and 4mm knitting needles
Large blunt-ended sewing needle
5 buttons, 2cm in diameter
40cm square feather cushion pad

Tension
22 stitches and 30 rows to 10cm square over stocking stitch using 4mm needles

Notes
Whenever you change colour, it is easier to weave in any loose yarn ends as you work. *See Masterclass, page 67.*

Fold along marked lines making sure buttonhole band is on top of button band.
Join side seams, sewing through all layers.
Sew buttons on button band to match buttonholes.
Insert cushion pad.

Stripe sequence
C 6 rows
B 7 rows
A 13 rows
B 6 rows
D 6 rows
B 3 rows
E 6 rows
B 6 rows
A 6 rows
B 3 rows
C 9 rows
Place marker at each end of last row for fold line
A 4 rows
B 1 row
C 9 rows
B 4 rows
D 4 rows
B 1 row
E 16 rows
B 3 rows
C 6 rows
B 7 rows
A 13 rows
B 6 rows
D 6 rows
B 3 rows
E 6 rows
B 6 rows
A 6 rows
B 3 rows
C 9 rows
Place marker at each end of last row for fold line
A 4 rows
B 1 row
C 9 rows
B 4 rows
D 4 rows
B 1 row
E 16 rows
B 3 rows
*C 6 rows
B 7 rows

To make the Stripe Cushion

Using 3.25mm needles and yarn C, cast on 88 sts and work 6 rows in k1, p1 rib as folls:
Row 1 (RS) * K1, p1, rep from * to end.
Row 2 * K1, p1, rep from * to end.
Change to yarn B and work 7 rows in k1, p1 rib as set.
Change to 4mm needles and yarn A, beg with a knit row cont in stocking stitch – knit one row and purl one row alternately – using the stripe sequence given until *.
Note, you have already worked the first 2 stripes in the rib band and are starting the third stripe.
Change to 3.25mm needles and yarn C, work 5 rows in k1, p1 rib as set, ending with RS facing for next row.
Buttonhole row 1 Rib 6 sts, cast off next 3 sts, [rib until 15 sts on RH needle, cast off next 3 sts] rep four times more, rib to end.
Buttonhole row 2 Change to yarn B, work across row in k1, p1 rib as set but cast on 3 sts over those cast off on previous row. *See Masterclass, opposite.*
With yarn B, work 5 more rows in k1, p1 rib.
Cast off in rib.

To finish

Weave in any loose yarn ends. *See Masterclass, page 67.*
Lay the work out flat and gently steam the finished piece on the reverse.

Masterclass

Making a buttonhole

There are several different types of buttonholes within knitting – horizontal, vertical, eyelet, yarn over to name a few. I have used just one method for all the projects within this book, the horizontal buttonhole made over two rows as it is a good, all-purpose method that suits both garments and homewares alike.

Buttonholes need to be spaced evenly so that the band will not gap when it is buttoned. Some patterns will say something like 'work six buttonholes evenly spaced', but it can be tricky to work it all out correctly if you are having to guess how many rows between each buttonhole. In this cushion cover pattern I have taken all the guesswork out of spacing the buttonholes by putting them horizontally along two rows.

Match your buttons to the size of the buttonhole; as knitted fabric stretches, the button should be only just able to slip through the hole. If you are in any doubt, knit a sample swatch with a buttonhole to determine whether it is the correct size. A good rule of thumb is that a buttonhole should be two stitches smaller than the width of the button.

A horizontal buttonhole is made by casting off stitches on one row that are then offset by casting on the same amount of stitches on the following row. Unless otherwise specified in the pattern, the first cast off row of the buttonhole is worked on the right side of the piece. This is a very versatile technique as either fewer or more stitches can be cast off to vary the size of the buttonhole.

On the first row, work to the position of the buttonhole. Work two stitches and then lift the first stitch over the second one to cast off one stitch. Continue casting off the required number of stitches; for this cushion cover, it is three stitches for each buttonhole repeated at regular intervals along the row. Work to the end of the row. On the return row, work to the cast off stitches. Turn the work and put the tip of the right-hand needle between the first two stitches on the left-hand needle. Using the cable cast-on technique (see page 24–5), cast on the same number of stitches cast off on the previous row. Turn the work back and complete the row.

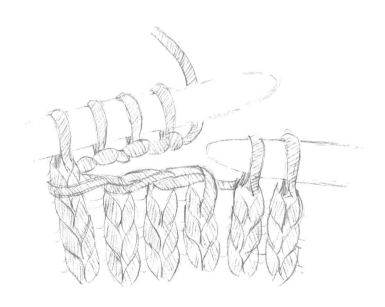

Stripe Throw

A deceptively simple throw that is worked in four easy sections, which are then pieced together. Knitted in the trinity of basic stitches – garter, stocking and reverse stocking stitch – this pattern really couldn't be easier. You could knit this throw in plain block colours, but for added interest I have introduced some elementary stripe sequences of varying complexity.

Skill level...

EASY

In this project you will learn...

Putting together a simple stripe sequence; following a colourwork chart

Stitches used...

Garter stitch; stocking stitch; reverse stocking stitch

Size
Finished size of throw once sewn: approximately 150cm square
Actual size of each knitted piece: approximately 75cm square

Materials
Light-weight DK wool yarn, such as
  Rowan Classic Baby Alpaca DK 3 LIGHT
    A 11 x 50g balls in light grey
    B 9 x 50g balls in dark grey
    C 8 x 50g balls in brown
Pair of 4mm knitting needles
Large blunt-ended sewing needle

Tension
22 stitches and 30 rows to 10cm square over stocking stitch using 4mm needles

Notes
Whenever you change colour, it is easier to weave in any loose yarn ends as you work.
See Masterclass, page 67.

To make the Stripe Throw

First square
three wide stripes using yarns A, B and C
Using yarn A cast on 165 sts and work 5cm in garter stitch – knit every row – ending with RS facing for next row. *You will have worked approx 20 rows.*
Cont in stocking stitch – knit one row and purl one row alternately – with garter stitch edge as folls:
Row 1 (RS) Knit.
Row 2 Purl to last 12 sts, k12.
Rep last 2 rows using yarn A until work measures 25cm from cast-on edge, ending with RS facing for next row. *You will have worked approx 60 stocking stitch rows in yarn A.*
Change to yarn B and rep rows 1 and 2 until work measures 50cm from cast-on edge ending with RS facing for next row. *You will have worked approx 74 stocking stitch rows in yarn B.*
Change to yarn C and rep rows 1 and 2 until work measures 75cm from cast-on edge, ending with RS facing for next row. *You will have worked approx 74 stocking stitch rows in yarn C.* Cast off.

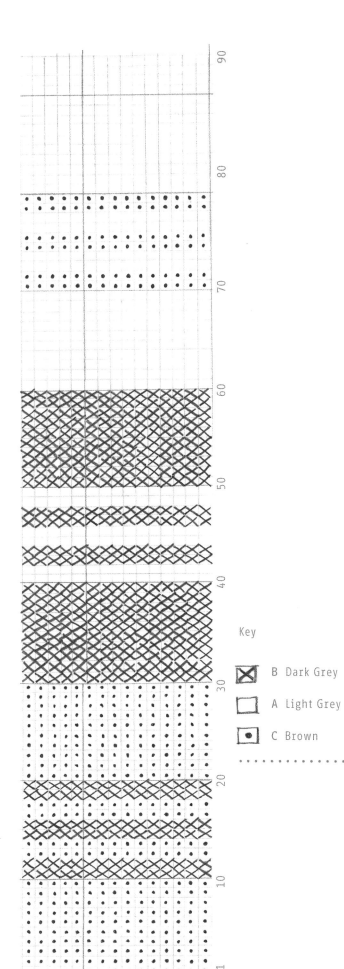

Second square
90-row stripe sequence using yarns A, B and C
C 10 rows
B 2 rows
C 2 rows
B 2 rows
C 2 rows
B 2 rows
C 10 rows
B 10 rows
A 2 rows
B 2 rows
A 2 rows
B 2 rows
A 2 rows
B 10 rows
A 10 rows
C 2 rows
A 2 rows
C 2 rows
A 2 rows
C 2 rows
A 10 rows

Using yarn B cast on 165 sts and work 5cm in garter stitch ending with RS facing for next row. *You will have worked approx 20 rows.*
Cont in stocking stitch with garter stitch edge, changing colour as given in stripe sequence above or shown in the chart opposite, as folls:

Key

⊠ B Dark Grey

☐ A Light Grey

⊡ C Brown

Masterclass

How to read a colourwork chart
Colourwork instructions can either be written out in full within the knitting pattern or represented as a chart on graph paper.
The different shades of yarn that make up the colourwork motif are represented either as a shaded colour (see page 46) or, as shown here, as a symbol.
With both types of colourwork chart, each square of the chart represents one stitch, and each line of squares represents one row. The right side rows (or odd numbered knit rows) are read from right to left, while the wrong side rows (or even numbered purl rows) are read from left to right. The rows of the chart are read from the bottom to the top.

Row 1 (RS) Knit.
Row 2 Purl to last 12 sts, k12.
Rep last 2 rows, keeping colour sequence correct, until work measures 75cm from cast-on edge, ending with RS facing for next row. Cast off.

Third square
16-row stripe repeat using yarns A, B and C
Stripe repeat to be worked throughout
C 3 rows
B 1 row
C 3 rows
A 9 rows

Using yarn C cast on 165 sts and work 5cm in garter stitch ending with RS facing for next row. *You will have worked approx 20 rows.*
Cont in stocking stitch with garter stitch edge, changing colour as given in stripe sequence above, as folls:
Row 1 (RS) Knit.
Row 2 Purl to last 12 sts, k12.
Rep last 2 rows, keeping colour sequence correct, until work measures 75cm from cast-on edge, ending with RS facing for next row. Cast off.

Fourth square
four-row stripe repeat using yarns A and B
Stripe repeat to be worked throughout
A 2 rows
B 2 rows

Using yarn A cast on 165 sts and work 5cm in garter stitch changing colour as given in stripe sequence above, ending with RS facing for next row. *You will have worked approx 20 rows.*
Cont in stocking stitch with garter stitch edge, keeping colour sequence correct, as folls:
Row 1 (RS) Knit.
Row 2 Purl to last 12 sts, k12.
Rep last 2 rows, keeping colour sequence correct, until work measures 39cm from cast-on edge, ending with RS facing for next row.
Keeping colour sequence correct, cont in reverse stocking stitch as folls:
Row 1 (RS) K12, purl to end.
Row 2 Knit.
Rep last 2 rows, keeping colour sequence correct, until work measures 75cm from cast-on edge, ending with RS facing for next row. Cast off.

To finish
Weave in any loose yarn ends. *See Masterclass, page 67.*
Lay the work out flat and gently steam the finished piece on the reverse.
Join the cast-off edge of the first square to the left selvedge of the fourth square.
Join the cast-off edge of the third square to the left selvedge of the second square.
Join these two strips together down the centre, as shown in the diagram below. *The arrows show the direction of the knitting, with the cast-on edge at the base and the cast-off edge at the tip of the arrow.*

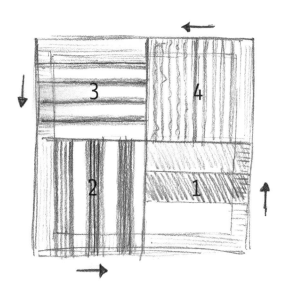

Pull-on Hats

Two essential winter hats – one plain beanie in stocking stitch with a roll edge, the other a basic 'New Yorker' style in simple k1, p1 rib. Both hats are made in luxurious alpaca yarns for maximum softness, comfort and warmth. These hats are easy to make with small amounts of decreasing so they are a great introduction to easy shaping techniques.

Skill level...

EASY

In this project you will learn...

Working simple shaping using decreases

Stitches used...

Stocking stitch; k1, p1 rib

Size
One size to fit average adult head

For the plain hat
Materials
2 x 100g skeins of medium-weight DK yarn, such as
  Blue Sky Alpacas Royal (4) MEDIUM
Pair of 5.5mm knitting needles
Large blunt-ended sewing needle

Tension
16 sts and 22 rows to 10cm square measured over stocking stitch using 5.5mm needles

For the rib hat
Materials
1 x 100g skein of light-weight DK yarn, such as
  Blue Sky Alpacas Worsted Hand Dyes (3) LIGHT
Pair of 4mm knitting needles
Large blunt-ended sewing needle

Tension
22 stitches and 30 rows to 10cm square measured over stocking stitch using 4mm needles

To knit the plain hat

Cast on 78 sts and beg with a knit row work 38 rows in stocking stitch – knit one row and purl one row alternately – ending with RS facing for next row.

Shape crown

Row 1 (RS) K8, [k2tog tbl, k1, k2tog, k14] 3 times, k2tog tbl, k1, k2tog, k8.
70 sts.

Row 2 and all WS rows Purl.

Row 3 K7, [k2tog tbl, k1, k2tog, k12] 3 times, k2tog tbl, k1, k2tog, k7.
62 sts.

Row 5 K6, [k2tog tbl, k1, k2tog, k10] 3 times, k2tog tbl, k1, k2tog, k6.
54 sts.

Row 7 K5, [k2tog tbl, k1, k2tog, k8] 3 times, k2tog tbl, k1, k2tog, k5.
46 sts.

Row 9 K4, [k2tog tbl, k1, k2tog, k6] 3 times, k2tog tbl, k1, k2tog, k4.
38 sts.

Row 11 K3, [k2tog tbl, k1, k2tog, k4] 3 times, k2tog tbl, k1, k2tog, k3.
30 sts.

Row 13 K2, [k2tog tbl, k1, k2tog, k2] 3 times, k2tog tbl, k1, k2tog, k2.
22 sts.

Row 15 K1, [k2tog tbl, k1, k2tog] 4 times, k1.
14 sts.

Cut working yarn leaving a long end, thread through remaining stitches, pull up and fasten off securely.

To knit the rib hat

Cast on 112 sts and work in k2, p2 rib until work measures 25cm from cast-on edge.

Shape crown

Next row (RS) [K2tog tbl, p2tog] to end.
56 sts.

Work 5 rows in k1, p1 rib.

Next row [K2tog tbl] to end.
28 sts.

Purl 1 row.

Next row [K2tog tbl] to end.
14 sts.

Cut working yarn leaving a long end, thread through remaining stitches, pull up and fasten off securely.

To finish

Weave in any loose yarn ends. *See Masterclass, page 67.*
Lay the work out flat and gently steam the reverse side of the finished piece, taking care not to flatten the rib.
Join the back seam using mattress stitch.
See Masterclass, page 40.

Masterclass

Simple shaping

The shaping of the crown for both these hats uses nothing more than the simplest method of decreasing – knitting two stitches together, so where you previously had two stitches on the needle, you now have only one.

Whenever I am designing, for ease I make sure that all the decreasing is done on a right side row. And preferably on a knit stitch, as most knitters find it easier to work a knit 2 together than a purl 2 together, especially when it comes to going through the back loops. (See pages 30–1.)

Whether you go through the front or back loops determines which direction the resulting stitch will slant towards. I like to incorporate such details into my designs, making it a feature. This is commonly known as fully fashioned shaping – we'll come back to this later on with the sweater and cardigan on pages 134–41.

Rag Bag

A useful bag made from strips of shirting fabric – either cloth store remnants or charity or thrift shop shirts – which are then cut into strips, knotted and knitted up in simple stocking stitch to create a circular bag with integral handles. As well as handling a less familiar knitting medium, with this bag project you will be mastering basic increasing. For ease and a neater finish, in my designs I always work the increase or decrease rows on a knit side.

Skill level...

EASY

In this project you will learn...

Creating and knitting with unusual yarns; increasing once knitwise

Stitches used...

Stocking stitch

Size
Finished size of bag once made up: approximately 35cm high (including handle) by 32cm in diameter
Actual size of knitted piece: approximately 46cm high (excluding handle) by 85cm wide

Materials
50 x 1.5m cut lengths of light-weight cotton fabric, each strip 2.5cm wide **(6)** SUPER BULKY
Pair of 10mm knitting needles
Large blunt-ended sewing needle

Tension
9 stitches and 12 rows to 10cm square measured over stocking stitch using 10mm needles

Masterclass

Making your own yarn from fabric
Knitting can be made up of any continuous length of yarn, and that includes strips of shirting fabric as used here. In the past I have used many different materials, even cut strips from plastic shopping bags.

Starting at one corner of the fabric, cut along one side 2.5cm in from the edge, but stopping when you are 2.5cm from the end. Next, make another cut in the opposite direction, 2.5cm from the previous cut and again stopping before you reach the end of the fabric. Continue making cuts in this way across the whole surface of the fabric. This will make one continuous 2.5cm wide length of fabric in a sort of spiral. Knot all the lengths of fabric together and wind into a ball. Now it is ready to be knitted up.

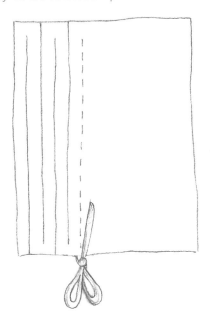

Masterclass

Increasing once knitwise

There are a few different methods you can use to make an extra stitch, this one is sometimes called a bar increase and is made by knitting into both the front and back of a single stitch.

Work to the position of the increase. Insert the right-hand needle knitwise into the stitch to be increased. Wrap the yarn anti-clockwise around the needle and pull it through as though knitting, but leave the stitch on the left-hand needle.

Insert the right-hand needle into the back of the same stitch on the left-hand needle. Wrap the yarn anti-clockwise around the needle and pull it through. Slip the original stitch from the left-hand needle. You now have two stitches on the right-hand needle.

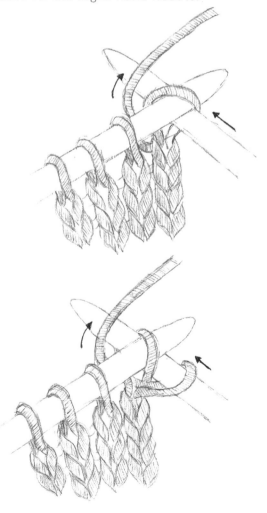

To make the Rag Bag

Cast on 5 sts.
Row 1 (RS) [inc in next stitch] 4 times, k1. *9 sts.*
Rows 2, 4, 6, 8, 10, 12, 14 and 16 Purl.
Row 3 [inc in next stitch] 8 times, k1. *17 sts.*
Row 5 [k1, inc in next stitch] 8 times, k1. *25 sts.*
Row 7 [k2, inc in next stitch] 8 times, k1. *33 sts.*
Row 9 [k3, inc in next stitch] 8 times, k1. *41 sts.*
Row 11 [k4, inc in next stitch] 8 times, k1. *49 sts.*
Row 13 [k5, inc in next stitch] 8 times, k1. *57 sts.*
Row 15 [k6, inc in next stitch] 8 times, k1. *65 sts.*
Row 17 [k7, inc in next stitch] 8 times, k1. *73 sts.*
Row 18 (WS) Knit. *This row makes a ridge.*
Beg with a knit row, cont in stocking stitch – knit one row and purl one row alternately – until work measures 35cm from the ridge, ending with RS facing for next row.
Work handles as folls:
Next row K12, cast off next 14 sts, knit next 21 sts, cast off next 14 sts, knit to end.
Next row P12, cast on 28 sts, purl next 21 sts, cast on 28 sts, purl to end. *101 sts.*
Next row Knit.
Next row Purl.
Cast off.

To finish

Weave in any loose yarn ends. *See Masterclass, page 67.*
Lay the work out flat and gently steam the reverse side of the finished piece.
Join the back seam using mattress stitch. *See Masterclass, page 40.*

10 Mittens

Practical mittens made in k2, p1 rib
and stocking stitch with a shaped
thumb and simple cast-off edge finish.
Made in a natural rare sheep breed
wool with a generous rib cuff, which
can either be turned down for a wrist-
length mitten or kept up to extend
way past the wrist so there's no gap
between coat sleeve and mitten!

Skill level...

■■□□ ▭

EASY

In this project you will learn...

Increasing twice knitwise; picking up stitches

Stitches used...

K2, p2 rib; stocking stitch

Size
One size to fit woman's average size hand

Materials
2 x 50g balls of light-weight DK wool yarn, such
    as Rowan British Sheeps Breed DK  LIGHT
Pair each of 4mm and 4.5mm knitting needles
Large blunt-ended sewing needle

Tension
22 stitches and 30 rows to 10cm square measured
over stocking stitch using 4mm needles

To knit the Mittens

Right mitten
Using 4.5mm needles cast on 44 sts and work in
rib as folls:
Row 1 (RS) * K2, p1, rep from * to last 2 sts, k2.
Row 2 P2, * k1, p2, rep from * to end.
Rep last 2 rows until work measures 13cm from
cast-on edge, ending with RS facing for next row.
Change to 4mm needles and cont in rib as set
until work measures 24cm from cast-on edge,
ending with RS facing for next row.
Cont in stocking stitch – knit one row and purl
one row alternately – as folls:
Shape thumb gusset
Row 1 (inc) K22, inc knitwise into next stitch,
k1, inc knitwise into next stitch, k19.
46 sts.
Row 2 Purl.
Row 3 Knit.
Row 4 Purl.
Row 5 (inc) K22, inc knitwise into next stitch,
k3, inc knitwise into next stitch, k19.
48 sts.
Cont to inc 1 st on each side of thumb gusset on
every 4th row until there are 56 sts.
Work 1 row straight.
Next row K37, turn.
Next row Inc twice knitwise into next stitch,
p15, turn.

Next row Inc twice knitwise into next stitch, k to end of row.
18 sts.
** Beg with a purl row, work 7 rows in stocking stitch.
Cast off.
Cut working yarn leaving a long end. *You will use to sew up the thumb seam.*
With RH needle rejoin yarn, pick up and knit 4 sts at base of thumb, knit to end of row.
46 sts.
Beg with a purl row work 17 rows stocking stitch, ending with RS facing for next row.
Cast off. **

Left Mitten
Work to match Right Mitten, reversing position of thumb gusset as folls:
Shape thumb gusset
Row 1 (inc) K19, inc knitwise into next stitch, k1, inc knitwise into next stitch, k22.
46 sts.
Row 2 Purl.
Row 3 Knit.
Row 4 Purl.
Row 5 K19, inc knitwise into next stitch, k3, knit into front and back of next stitch, k22.
Cont to inc 1 st at each side of thumb gusset on every 4th row until there are 56 sts.
Work 1 row straight.
Next row K34, turn.
Next row Inc twice knitwise into next stitch, p15, turn.
Next row Inc twice knitwise into next stitch, k to end.
18 sts.
Complete as given for Right Mitten from ** to **.

To finish
Weave in any loose yarn ends. *See Masterclass, page 67.*
Lay the work out flat and gently steam the reverse side of the finished piece, taking care not to flatten the rib.
Join the side seam using mattress stitch.
See Masterclass, page 38.

Masterclass

Increasing twice knitwise
Occasionally, within a row you will need to increase by more than one stitch at a time, such as when knitting the thumb gusset of these mittens. Increasing twice knitwise is worked using exactly the same principle are increasing once knitwise but obviously you end up with more stitches.

Work to the position of the increase. Insert the right-hand needle knitwise into the front of the stitch to be increased. Wrap the yarn anti-clockwise around the needle and pull it through as if knitting, but leave the stitch on the left-hand needle.

Insert the right-hand needle into the back of the same stitch on the left-hand needle. Wrap the yarn anti-clockwise around the needle and pull it through.

Knit into the front of the same stitch as before. Then slip the original stitch from the left-hand needle. You now have three stitches on the right-hand needle.

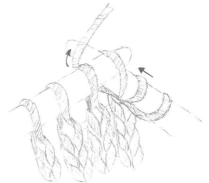

11 Round Cushion

This deceptively simple round cushion, made in timeless linen yarn and finished with a natural horn button, uses a technique called short row shaping. Before completing a full row of stitches, you turn, wrap the end stitch and continue in the opposite direction, hence the term short row. Some designers hide the wraps made at each turning point, however, I love the effect they give and prefer to incorporate them into the design.

Skill level...

INTERMEDIATE

In this project you will learn...

Short row shaping

Stitches used...

Stocking stitch

Size
Finished size of cushion once made up:
approximately 38cm diameter by 8cm deep
Actual size of knitted piece: 44cm diameter

Materials
3 x 50g balls of light-weight DK linen yarn, such as Rowan Lenpur Linen **3** LIGHT
Pair of 4mm knitting needles
40cm diameter round feather cushion pad
Large blunt-ended sewing needle
2 four-hole buttons, 2.5cm diameter

Tension
22 stitches and 30 rows to 10cm square measured over stocking stitch using 4mm needles

To make the Round Cushion
Make two pieces the same
Cast on 44 sts.
Work in stocking stitch – knit one row and purl one row alternately – and short rows as folls:
Row 1 Knit to end.
Row 2 Purl to end.
Row 3 Knit 42 sts, wrap next stitch, turn.
See Masterclass on short row shaping, overleaf.
Row 4 Purl to end.
Row 5 Knit 40 sts, wrap next stitch, turn.
Row 6 Purl to end.
Cont working in short rows as set, leaving 2 sts more unworked on every knit row until there are no more sts to knit.
This completes the first segment of the circle.
Beg again with Row 1 and cont until 8 segments have been worked to form a full circle.
Do not cast off sts, but join last segment to first segment by grafting one stitch from the needle with the corresponding stitch on the cast-on edge. *See page 41.*

To finish
Weave in any loose yarn ends. *See Masterclass, page 67.*
Lay the work out flat and gently steam the reverse side of the finished piece.
Join two pieces together around the curved edges using back stitch, leaving an opening for inserting the cushion pad.
Insert the cushion pad and neatly sew the opening to close.
Take a thread and gently gather together the small hole in the centre and sew a button to both front and back of cushion. Fasten securely.

Masterclass

Short row shaping

Short rows are partial rows of knitting that create a curve or other shape. The result is that one side or section has more rows that the other, but no stitches are decreased. This technique is sometimes called 'turning' because the work is turned within the row. Short rows can be worked on one or both sides of a piece at the same time. Shaping with short rows creates a smoother shape and eliminates the jagged edges that occur when you cast off a series of stitches such as at shoulder or on collars.

   When the instructions for any row say 'turn', this means that the remaining stitches are not worked. To avoid creating a hole when turning on a knit row, work a wrap stitch as folls:

Wrapping a knit stitch

1 Work up to the 'turn'. With the yarn to the back of the work, slip the stitch purlwise on to the right-hand needle.
2 Bring the yarn forward between the two needles so that it is sitting at the front of the work.
3 Slip the same stitch back on to the left-hand needle and take the yarn back between the two needles. Turn the work. One stitch is wrapped and you are ready to continue the next row.

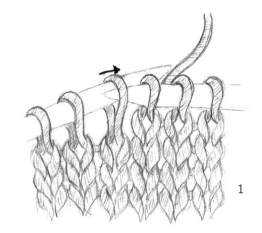

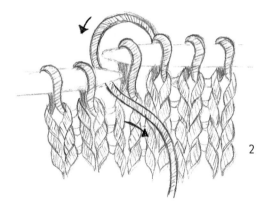

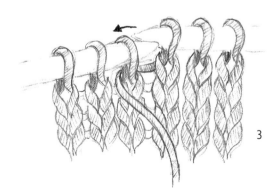

12 Two-needle Socks

An introduction to knitting socks – something every new knitter should try to master. Cosy and comfortable, these chunky socks are the perfect accompaniment for the now classic Ugg boot. Using basic k1, p1 rib and stocking stitch, short row shaping forms the heel while fully fashioned decreasing gives a professional finish to the toe.

Skill level...

INTERMEDIATE

In this project you will learn...

Fully fashioned decreasing; short row shaping

Stitches used...

K1, p1 rib; stocking stitch

Size
Finished size of socks once made up:
to fit women's average shoe size 4–6 (see note)
Actual size of knitted piece:
40cm high by 21cm wide

Materials
3 x 50g balls of medium-weight aran wool yarn, such as Rowan Cashsoft Aran (4) MEDIUM
Pair each of 4mm and 4.5mm knitting needles
Large blunt-ended sewing needle

Tension
19 stitches and 25 rows to 10cm square over stocking stitch using 4.5mm needles

Note
You can adjust the length of the sock to make it suitable for either a smaller or larger shoe size by working more or fewer rows straight after the heel shaping.

Masterclass

Fully fashioned shaping
Fully fashioning is a technique whereby the increase and decrease stitches for the shaping within a project are used deliberately for decorative effect, as seen in the toe of this simple sock. Both increase and decrease stitches slope in certain directions, so this can be incorporated as an integral part of a design. When working fully fashioned shaping, the increases and decreases are usually worked three stitches in from the edges of the work so that they are visible once the piece has been sewn up.

To increase at each end of a knit row:
K3, make 1 stitch by picking up the horizontal loop before the next stitch and working into the back of it, k to last 3 sts, make 1 st as before, k3.

To decrease at each end of a knit row:
K3, k2tog tbl, k to last 5 sts, k2tog, k3.

To decrease at each end of a purl row:
P3, p2tog, p to last 5 sts, p2tog tbl, p3.

To make the Two Needle Socks
Make two the same

Using 4mm needles cast on 40 sts and work 6.5cm in knit 1, purl 1 rib.

Change to 4.5mm needles and cont in rib as set until work measures 12.5cm from cast-on edge.

Beg with a knit row, work in stocking stitch – knit one row and purl one row alternately – until work measures 19.5cm from cast-on edge, ending with RS facing for next row.

Shape heel
Row 1 (RS) K13, wrap next stitch, turn.
See Masterclass on short row shaping, page 105.
Row 2 and all following WS rows Purl.
Row 3 K12, wrap next stitch, turn.
Row 5 K11, wrap next stitch, turn.
Row 7 K10, wrap next stitch, turn.
Row 9 K9 sts, wrap next stitch, turn.
Row 11 K8, wrap next stitch, turn.
Row 13 K7, wrap next stitch, turn.
Row 15 K6, wrap next stitch, turn.
Row 17 K5, wrap next stitch, turn.
Row 19 K6, wrap next stitch, turn.
Row 21 K7, wrap next stitch, turn.
Row 23 K8, wrap next stitch, turn.
Row 25 K9, wrap next stitch, turn.
Row 27 K10, wrap next stitch, turn.
Row 29 K11, wrap next stitch, turn.
Row 31 K12, wrap next stitch, turn.
Row 33 K13, wrap next stitch, turn.
Row 35 Knit across ALL stitches.
Row 36 P13, wrap next stitch, turn.
Row 37 and all foll RS rows Knit.
Row 38 P12, wrap next stitch, turn.
Row 40 P11, wrap next stitch, turn.
Row 42 P10, wrap next stitch, turn.
Row 44 P9, wrap next stitch, turn.
Row 46 P8, wrap next stitch, turn.
Row 48 P7, wrap next stitch, turn.
Row 50 P6, wrap next stitch, turn.
Row 52 P5, wrap next stitch, turn.
Row 54 P6, wrap next stitch, turn.
Row 56 P7, wrap next stitch, turn.
Row 58 P8, wrap next stitch, turn.
Row 60 P9, wrap next stitch, turn.
Row 62 P10, wrap next stitch, turn.
Row 64 P11, wrap next stitch, turn.
Row 66 P12, wrap next stitch, turn.
Row 68 P13, wrap next stitch, turn.
Row 70 Purl across ALL stitches and place marker

at each end of row.

Beg with a knit row cont in stocking stitch until work measures 12.5cm from markers, ending with RS facing for next row.

Adjust the length of sock here by working more or fewer rows straight.

Shape toe
Row 1 (RS) K7, k2tog, k2, k2tog tbl, k14, k2tog, k2, k2tog tbl, k7.
36 sts.
Row 2 and all following WS rows Purl.
Row 3 K6, k2tog, k2, k2tog tbl, k12, k2tog, k2, k2tog tbl, k6.
32 sts.
Row 5 K5, k2tog, k2, k2tog tbl, k10, k2tog, k2, k2tog tbl, k5.
28 sts.
Row 7 K4, k2tog, k2, k2tog tbl, k8, k2tog, k2, k2tog tbl, k4.
24 sts.
Row 9 K3, k2tog, k2, k2tog tbl, k6, k2tog, k2, k2tog tbl, k3.
20 sts.
Row 11 K2, k2tog, k2, k2tog tbl, k4, k2tog, k2, k2tog tbl, k2.
16 sts.
Row 12 Purl.
Cast off.

To finish
Weave in any loose yarn ends. *See Masterclass, page 67.*

Lay the work out flat and gently steam the reverse side of the finished piece, taking care not to flatten the rib.

Starting at the toe, join the long seam using mattress stitch (see page 38) but reversing the seam at the turnover part of the rib (the section worked on 4mm needles).

Oversew the toe seam on the right side.

13 Four-needle Socks

A classic pair of stripey socks, for either a man or a woman, worked on four needles. These socks are much easier to knit than they look as the yarn is a fine self-striping wool, so there is no need for any tricky colour changes. This design is finished using Kitchener stitch to give a neat, flat toe and very professional finish.

Skill level...

◼◼◼◻

EXPERIENCED

In this project you will learn...

Knitting in the round on four needles; finishing a sock toe with Kitchener stitch

Stitches used...

Stocking stitch

Size
To fit (shoe size)

UK 7–9	10–13	1–3	4–6	7–9	10–12
EUR 24–27	28–32	33–36	37–40	41–43	44–47

Materials
2 (2: 2: 2: 2: 2) x 50g balls of fine 4ply wool blend yarn, such as Regia Erika Knight Design Line Sock Yarn (**2**) FINE
Set of four 2.75mm double-pointed needles
Tapestry needle

Tension
30 stitches and 12 rows to 10cm square measured over stocking stitch using 2.75mm needles

Special abbreviations
Sl1k slip one stitch knitwise
Sl1p slip one stitch purlwise

To make the Four Needle Socks
Make two the same
Cast on 48 (52: 56: 60: 64: 68) sts.
Divide stitches between three needles and join by sliding last stitch onto same needles as first.
Slide a stitch marker onto the needle to mark beginning of round.

Rib cuff
Round 1 [K1, p1] rep to end.
Rep Round 1 until work measures 15 (16: 17: 18: 19: 20)cm.

Heel flap
K12, (13: 14: 15: 16: 17), turn.
Row 1 Sl1p, p23 (25: 27: 29: 31: 33), turn.
24 (26: 28: 30: 32: 34) sts on this needle.
Slide rem sts on to spare needle.
Row 2 Sl1k, k23 (25: 27: 29: 31: 33), turn.
Working back and forth on these 24 (26: 28: 30: 32: 34) sts.
Rep last two rows 10 (11: 12: 13: 14: 15) more times.

Heel shaping
Row 1 Sl1p, p12 (14: 16: 16: 18: 18), p2tog, p1, turn.
Row 2 Sl1k, k3 (5: 6: 5: 6: 5), k2tog tbl, turn.
Row 3 Sl1p, p4 (6: 7: 6: 7: 6), p2tog, p1, turn.
Row 4 Sl1k, k5 (7: 8: 7: 8: 7), k2tog tbl, k1, turn.
Cont in this manner, taking in one more stitch

each row as set, until all the heel flap stitches have been included.

Pick up for instep
Pick up and knit 12 (13: 14: 15: 16: 17) sts down side of heel flap, k24 (26: 28: 30: 32: 34) sts from cuff, pick up and knit 12 (13: 14: 15: 16: 17) sts up side of heel flap, k7 (8: 9: 9: 10: 10). 62 (68: 74: 78: 84: 88) sts ending at marker.

Shape instep
Round 1 K17 (19: 21: 22: 24: 25), k2tog, k2tog, k24 (26: 28: 30: 32: 34), k2tog tbl, knit to end.
60 (66: 72: 76: 82: 86) sts.
Round 2 Knit to end of round.
Round 3 K16 (18: 20: 21: 23: 24), k2tog, k24 (26: 28: 30: 32: 34), k2tog tbl, knit to end.
58 (64: 70: 74: 80: 84) sts.
Round 4 Knit to end of round.
Cont in this manner, dec 2 sts on every alt row as set, until 48 (52: 56: 60: 64: 68) sts rem.

Foot
Next round Knit to end of round.
Rep this round until foot measures 14 (16: 18: 20: 22.5: 24.5)cm from back of heel.

Decrease for toe
Round 1 K9 (10: 11: 12: 13: 14), k2tog, k2, k2tog tbl, k18 (20: 22: 24: 26: 28), k2tog, k2, k2tog tbl, knit to end of round.
Round 2 Knit to end of round.
Round 3 K8 (9: 10: 11: 12: 13), k2tog, k2, k2tog tbl, k16 (18: 20: 22: 24: 26), k2tog, k2, k2tog tbl, knit to end of round.
Round 4 Knit to end of round.
Cont in this manner, dec 4 sts on every alt round as set, until 24 (28: 28: 32: 32: 36) sts rem.
Next round K18 (21: 21: 24: 24: 27).
Rearrange stitches so first 6 (7: 7: 8: 8: 9) sts and last 6 (7: 7: 8: 8: 9) sts of round are on one needle with the remaining 12 (14: 14: 16: 16: 18) sts on another needle.

To finish
Graft toe together using Kitchener stitch. *See Masterclass, opposite.*
Weave in any loose yarn ends. *See Masterclass, page 67.*
Lay the work out flat and gently steam the reverse side of the finished piece, taking care not to flatten the rib.

Masterclass

Grafting a sock toe using Kitchener stitch

Cut the working yarn leaving a 30cm tail. Thread through a tapestry needle.

Hold the two remaining knitting needles together, parallel to one another. With the knitting needle from which the long tail comes from at the back, insert the tapestry needle knitwise into the first stitch on the back needle.

Pull the yarn through, leaving the stitch on the needle.

1 * Insert tapestry needle knitwise into first stitch on front needle and slip stitch off needle.
2 Insert tapestry needle purlwise into next stitch on front needle. Pull yarn through, leaving stitch on needle.
3 Insert tapestry needle purlwise into first stitch on back needle and slip stitch off needle.
4 Insert tapestry needle knitwise into next stitch on back needle. Pull yarn through, leaving stitch on needle.
5 Repeat from * until all stitches have been grafted.
6 Secure end on inside of sock.

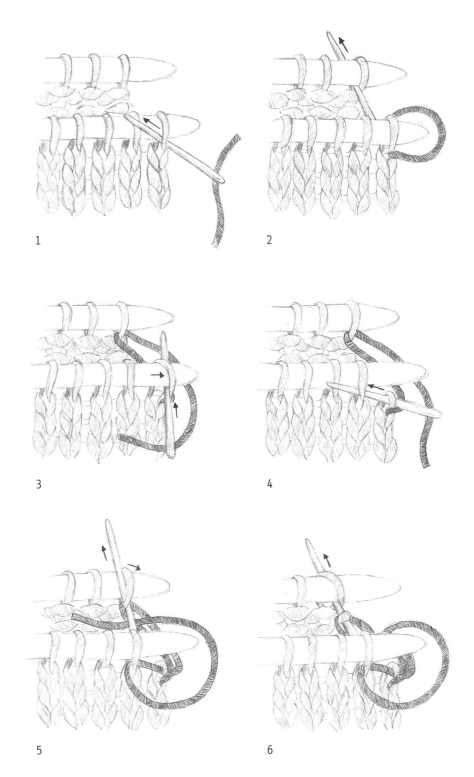

1

2

3

4

5

6

14 Cable Scarf

A long, long scarf knitted in super bulky yarn on super chunky knitting needles, this design incorporates an oversized cable stitch with a neat selvedge edge. This is the perfect project for a novice to tackle cables because by working in such chunky wool on large needles the cable stitches are clearly visible, so you will be able to see the cable taking shape as you knit.

Skill level...

■■■■
EXPERIENCED

In this project you will learn...
How to work a cable

Stitches used...

Stocking stitch: reverse stocking stitch: cable C12B

Size
Approximately 23cm wide by 230cm long, depending on your tension

Materials
5 x 100g balls of super bulky wool yarn, such as Rowan Big Wool **(4)** SUPER BULKY
Pair of 12mm knitting needles
Cable needle

Tension
9 stitches and 12 rows to 10cm square measured over stocking stitch using 12mm needles

Special abbreviation
C12B cable 12 back – slip next 6 sts onto cable needle and hold at back of work, k6 from LH needle, then k6 from cable needle

To make the Cable scarf
Cast on 26 sts and work in rib as folls:
Rib row 1 (RS) [K2, p1] to last 2 sts, k2.
Rib row 2 [P2, k1] to last 2 sts, p2.
Rep last 2 rows until work measures 23cm, ending with RS facing for next row.
Now work in cable patt as folls:
Row 1 (RS) K2, p5, k12, p5, k2.
Row 2 P2, k5, p12, k5, p2.
Row 3 K2, p5, C12B, p5, k2.
Row 4 As row 2.
Rows 5–16 Rep rows 1 and 2 six times more.
Rep these 16 rows 11 times more, then work rows 1–6, ending with RS facing for next row.
Rep rib rows 1 and 2 until rib measures 23cm, ending with RS facing for next row. Cast off in rib.

To finish
Weave in any loose yarn ends. *See Masterclass, page 67.*
Lay the work out flat and gently steam the finished piece on the reverse.

Masterclass

How to knit a cable

Cables are made by swapping over, or
crossing, groups of stitches within a row using
a third short needle, known as a cable needle.
Originating from the islands of Scotland, they
are a traditional form of decorative knitting
known as Aran. Whilst it may look complex,
cabling is actually deceptively simple. The
cabling technique shown here can be done
with any number of stitches, such as in the
Cable Plait Hottie Cover on pages 118–21
where it is worked over 8 stitches instead of
12. Holding the cable needle to the back of the
work makes a cable that twists to the right.
To make a cable that twists to the left, simply
hold the cable need to the front of the work.

Cable 12 back (C12B)

Work to the position of the cable. Slip the
first six cable stitches purlwise off the left-
hand needle and onto the cable needle. Leave
the cable needle at the back of the work, then
knit the next six stitches on the left-hand
needle, keeping the yarn tight to prevent
a gap forming in the knitting. Knit the six
stitches directly from the cable needle, or if
preferred, slip the six stitches from the cable
needle back onto the left-hand needle and then
knit them. This completes the cable cross.

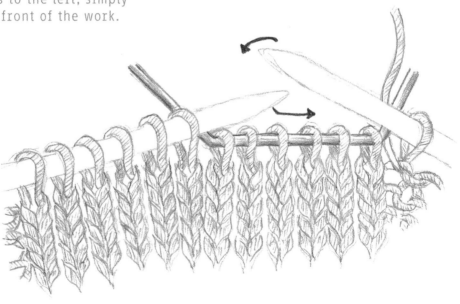

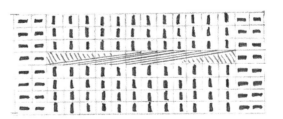

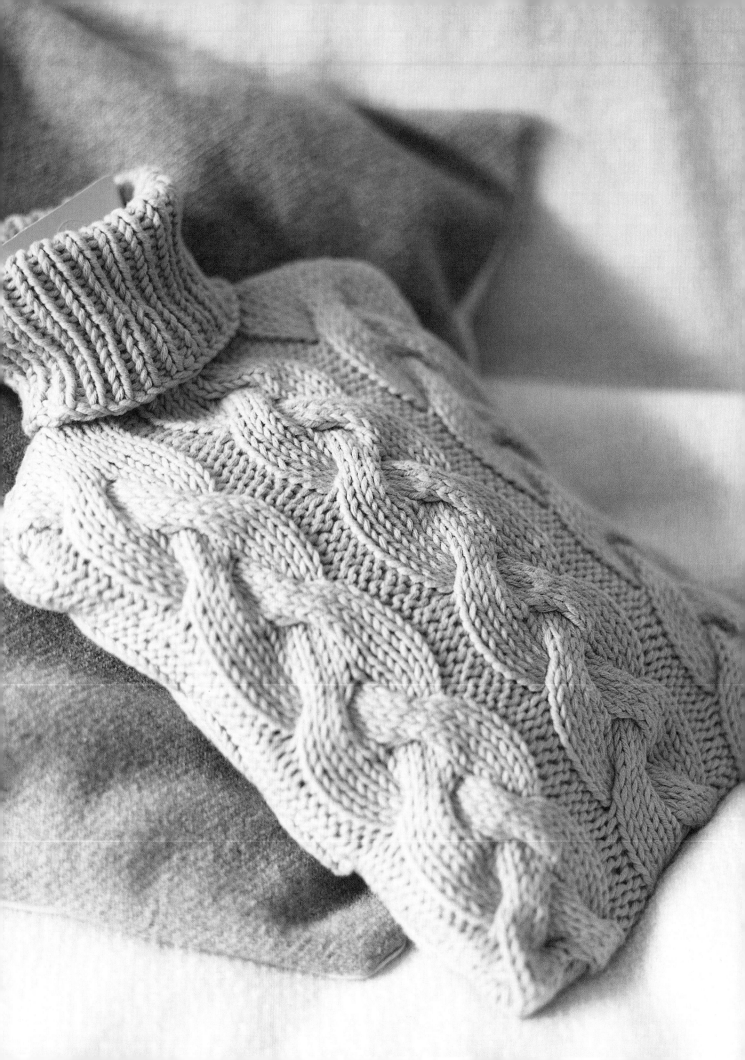

15 Cable Plait Hottie Cover

Dress up your hot water bottle with this elegant yet practical knitted cover. Made in soft, natural cotton, the stylish cable plait stitch design is finished with a contrasting rib polo neck.

Skill level...

INTERMEDIATE

In this project you will learn...
Working a cable plait

Stitches used...
Stocking stitch; k1, p1 rib; cable plait stitch

Size
One size to fit average size hotwater bottle
Actual size of knitted piece: 33cm high by 20cm wide

Materials
3 x 50g balls medium-weight aran cotton yarn, such as Debbie Bliss Eco Fairtrade Cotton
(4) MEDIUM
Pair each of 4mm and 4.5mm knitting needles
4.5mm cable needle
Large blunt-ended sewing needle

Tension
18 stitches and 24 rows to 10cm square measured over stocking stitch using 4.5mm needles

Special abbreviation
C8F cable 8 front – slip next 4 stitches onto cable needle and hold at front of work, knit 4 stitches from LH needle, then knit 4 stitches from cable needle.
C8B cable 8 back – slip next 4 stitches onto cable needle and hold at back of work, knit 4 stitches from LH needle, then knit 4 stitches from cable needle.

Masterclass

How to knit a cable plait
Worked over 12 stitches, the right 8 stitches are twisted to the right (C4B) while the left 4 stitches are knitted plain then the right 4 stitches are knitted plain while the left 8 stitches are twisted to the left (C4F). The result is a staggered combination of the two eight stitch cables, which results in a wonderful plait effect.

It is possible to make cables travel all over a piece of knitting by taking the cable stiches in any direction you wish. Just keep crossing over the stitches and making them travel across the knitting.

Why not work this pattern using any of the other cable stitches given in the Stitch Library (see pages 58–9).

To make the Cable Plait Hottie Cover
Front
Using 4mm needles cast on 48 sts and work 8 rows in k1, p1 rib as folls:
Rib row 1 (RS) [K1, p1] to end.
Rib row 2 [K1, p1] to end.
Rep last 2 rows three more times, ending with RS facing for next row.
Change to 4.5mm needles and work in cable patt as folls:
Row 1 (RS) P3, [k12, p3] to end of row.
Row 2 K3, [p12, k3] to end of row.
Row 3 P3, [C8F, k4, p3] to end of row.
Row 4 K3, [p12, k3] to end of row.
Row 5 P3, [k12, p3] to end of row.
Row 6 K3, [p12, k3] to end of row.
Row 7 P3, [k12, p3] to end of row.
Row 8 K3, [p12, k3] to end of row.
Row 9 P4, [k4, C8B, p3] to end of row.
Row 10 K3, [p12, k3] to end of row.
Row 11 P3, [k12, p3] to end of row.
Row 12 K3, [p12, k3] to end of row.
Rep 12 row cable pattern 7 times.
84 rows worked; measures 36cm from cast-on edge.

Shape top
Keeping patt correct, cast off 4 sts at beg of next 4 rows, then cast off 3 sts at beg of next 2 rows. *26 sts.*
Change to 4mm needles and work 14 cm in k1, p1 rib.
Cast off in rib.

Back
Work as given for Front but rep 12-row cable patt 3 times.
36 rows worked; measures 16cm from cast-on edge.
Shape top as given for Front.

To finish
Weave in any loose yarn ends. *See Masterclass, page 67.*
Lay the work out flat and gently steam the finished piece on the reverse, taking care not to flatten the cables.
With RS together, pin the back and front together matching from the top.
Fold the front 13cm from the cast-on edge towards the back. This will overlap the back.
Pin through all layers.
Using mattress stitch (see page 38) join the first 7cm of rib, then cont in back stitch and sew all round cover, ensuring that you sew through all three layers where they overlap. Use mattress stitch for the last 7cm of rib. (This reverses the seam for the 'polo neck' of the hottie cover.)
Turn cover right side out and slip the hot water bottle inside.

16 Colour Block Throw

This is my simple take on the basic 'squares' blanket, a favourite project for beginner knitters. This patchwork throw is worked in one piece, so it requires no finishing other than weaving in a few yarn ends. This project introduces the technique called colour blocking, or intarsia, where a new thread of yarn is used for each colour change. Knitted in stocking stitch, this graphic throw is made in an aran-weight cotton to give good stitch clarity as well as year-round comfort.

Skill level...

INTERMEDIATE

In this project you will learn...

Changing colour yarns neatly using the colour block or intarsia method

Stitches used...

Stocking stitch

Size
Finished size of intarsia throw once made up:
approximately 120cm wide by 144cm long
Actual size of each colour block:
24cm wide by 24cm high

Materials
Medium-weight aran yarn, such as Debbie Bliss
  Eco Fairtrade Cotton 4 MEDIUM
    A 11 x 50g balls in black
    B 11 x 50g balls in beige
4.5mm circular knitting needle, 100cm long
Large blunt-ended sewing needle

Tension
18 stitches and 24 rows to 10cm square over stocking stitch using 4.5mm needles

Notes
Use a separate ball for each colour and twist the yarns on the wrong side of the fabric when changing colour to avoid a hole. *See Masterclass, overleaf.* Where possible, weave in any loose yarn ends as you work. *See Masterclass, page 67.*

Masterclass

Changing yarn using the intarsia method

When knitting using several colours across a row organise the yarns into 'bobbins' – small windings of individual yarns. To work out how much yarn you will need, calculate the number of stitches in that specific area then twist the yarn around the knitting needle that number of times, adding a small amount more for sewing in the ends. Once you have measured out the correct amount of yarn, either wind it into a small bobbin by hand or wrap it around a shop-bought bobbin.

1 To join in a new colour on a knit row, work up to the colour change. Drop the old colour. Pick up the new colour from under the old colour and knit to the next colour change.
2 On a purl row, work up to the colour change. Drop the old colour. Pick up the new colour from under the old colour and purl to the next colour change.

In effect, you are 'twisting' the two colour yarns to link them together. Be careful not to overtwist the yarn or the fabric will not lie flat. The object is the link together the two separate colour sections so that they form a single fabric.

To make the Colour Block Throw

Cast on 210 sts in the following colour sequence: 42A, 42B, 42A, 42B, 42A.

* First row of squares
Row 1 K42A, k42B, k42A, k42B, k42A.
Row 2 P42A, p42B, p42A, p42B, p42A.
These two rows set the squares for the first section of the throw. Work a further 54 rows. Cut yarn for each square leaving a length of about 15cm.

Second row of squares
Row 1 K42B, k42A, k42B, k42A, k42B.
Row 2 P42B, p42A, p42B, p42A, p42B.
These two rows set the squares for the second section of the throw. Work a further 54 rows. Cut yarn for each square leaving a length of about 15cm.
Rep from * twice more.
Six sections of squares have been worked.
Cast off, twisting yarns as the colours change.

To finish

Weave in any loose yarn ends. *See Masterclass, page 67.*
Lay the work out flat and gently steam the finished piece on the reverse.

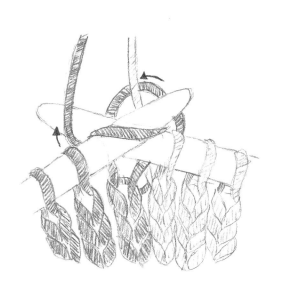

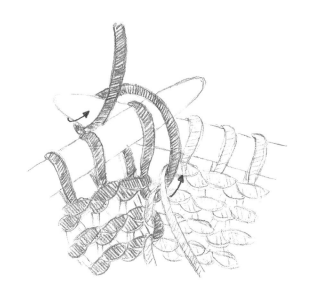

17 Fair Isle Pin Cushion

A small starter project to experiment with the 'stranding' or Fair Isle technique, which involves knitting with two different colour yarns across a row whilst following a simple stitch chart. Worked in contrasting black and white as a parody of the traditional Victorian-style lace patterns, this pin cushion is perfect for keeping your sewing materials in order.

Skill level...

■■■■▭
EXPERIENCED

In this project you will learn...

Working with two colours in one row – stranding and weaving; making a picot edging

Stitches used...

Stocking stitch

Size
Finished size of pin cushion once made up:
approx 6cm high by 12cm wide
Actual size of knitted pieces:
approx 6cm high by 12cm wide

Materials
Fine-weight 4ply mercerised cotton yarn,
  such as Yeomans Cotton Cannele (2) FINE
  25g of each of the following
    A black
    B ecru
Pair of 2.75mm knitting needles
Large blunt-ended sewing needle
Small amount of stuffing

Tension
32 stitches and 42 rows to 10cm square over stocking stitch using 2.75mm needles

To make the Pin Cushion
Front
Using yarn A cast on 41 sts and beg with a knit row work 10 rows in stocking stitch.
Work the 11 rows from the fair isle chart below, repeating the centre 12 stitches three times and ending WS facing for next row, cut yarn B.
Using yarn A and beg with a purl row, work 10 rows in stocking stitch, ending WS facing for next row. Cast off in purl.

Back
Using yarn A cast on 41 sts and beg with a knit row work 31 rows in stocking stitch, ending WS facing for next row. Cast off in purl.

Simple picot edging
Using yarn A cast on 5 sts. * Cast off 4 sts, slip remaining stitch on RH needle onto LH needle, cast on 4 sts; rep from * until edging measures 42cm. Cast off.

To finish
Weave in any loose yarn ends. *See Masterclass, page 67.*
Lay the work out flat and gently steam the finished piece on the reverse.
Join three sides, leaving one side open for stuffing. Stuff firmly and close seam.
Sew edging round pin cushion along seamline.

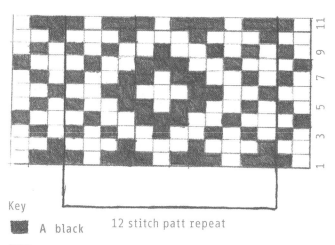

Key
■ A black
▭ B ecru
12 stitch patt repeat

Masterclass

Stranding

When knitting with two or more colours, if there is more than three stitches between each use of a colour, you need to strand the yarn across the back of the knitted fabric. This is to keep the threads tidy and prevent the fabric from puckering.

I have consciously designs this pin cushion a simple Fair Isle, ensuring that there are no more than three stitches between each use of a colour. This means the yarns can simply be carried across the back of the fabric.

1 On a knit row, drop the working yarn. Bring the new colour over the top of the dropped yarn and work to the next colour change.
2 Drop the working yarn. Bring the new colour under the dropped yarn and work to the next colour change. Repeat these two steps for all subsequent colour changes.

1 On a purl row, drop the working yarn. Bring the new colour over the top of the dropped yarn and work to the next colour change.
2 Drop the working yarn. Bring the new colour under the dropped yarn and work to the next colour change. Repeat these two steps for all subsequent colour changes.

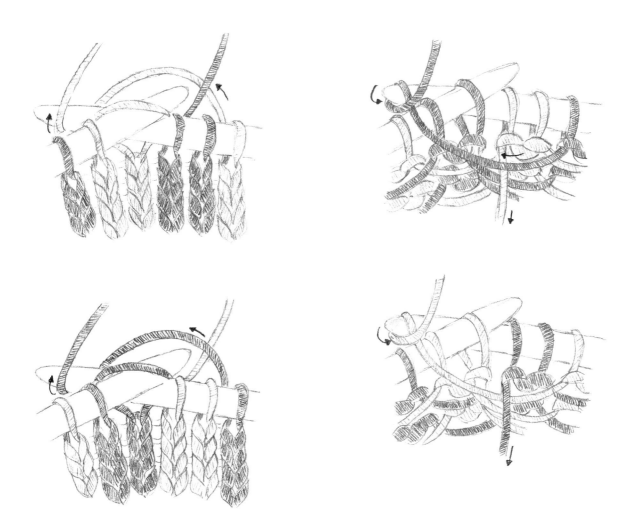

18 Rose Tea Cosy

A basic tea cosy shape knitted in stocking stitch decorated with a pretty rose design worked in muted vintage colours. For ease, the base colour of the rose motif is knitted using the intarsia method, while the extra highlights and shading are embroidered over the top with duplicate stitch. Apart from the three main colours, only small amounts of the other shades are needed, so this is the perfect project for using up scrap or stash yarns.

Skill level...

EXPERIENCED

In this project you will learn...

Adding colour using Swiss darning or duplicate stitch; colour blocking; reading from a chart

Stitches used...

Stocking stitch

Size
Finished size of tea cosy once made up: to fit average size teapot

Materials
DK-weight wool yarn, such as Rowan Cashsoft DK **(4)** MEDIUM

or

Patons Merino Deluxe DK **(4)** MEDIUM

- A 2 x 50g balls in stone (Rowan Cashsoft DK)
- B 1 x 50g ball in pink (Rowan Cashsoft 4ply, two strands used together)
- C 1 x 50g ball in ecru (Rowan Cashsoft DK)
- D 1 x 50g ball in taupe (Patons Merino Deluxe DK)
- E 1 x 50g ball in dark grey (Rowan Cashsoft DK)
- F 1 x 50g ball in purple (Patons Merino Deluxe DK)
- G 1 x 50g ball in amethyst (Rowan Kidsilk Haze, three strands used together)
- H 1 x 50g ball in brown (Rowan Cashsoft DK)
- I 1 x 50g ball in mid grey (Rowan Pure Wool DK)
- J 1 x 50g ball in teal (Rowan Cashsoft DK)
- K 1 x 50g ball in gold (Rowan Cashsoft DK)

Pair each of 3.25mm and 4mm knitting needles
0.5m wadding
0.5m fabric, for lining
Small piece of woven tape, approximately 10cm
Large blunt-ended sewing needle

Tension
22 stitches and 30 rows to 10cm square over stocking stitch using 4mm needles

Notes

To make the Tea Cosy
Front
Using 3.25mm needles and yarn B cast on 70 sts and work 4 rows in k1, pl 1 rib. Change to yarn A and work 1 row rib.
Change to yarn B and work 4 rows rib.
Change to 4mm needles and yarn A and beg with a knit row work 36 rows straight, ending with WS facing for next row and AT THE SAME TIME refer to chart overleaf and work the colours, as shown.
Use the colour blocking or intarsia technique. See Masterclass, page 124.
Note: do not work the bud design indicated in the dotted box. This is to be worked on the back only.
Next row Dec 1 st at each end of next row. *68 sts*
Work 3 rows straight.
Next row Dec 1 st at each end of next row. *66 sts*
Work 2 rows straight.
Next row Dec 1 st at each end of next and every alt row until 58 sts remain.

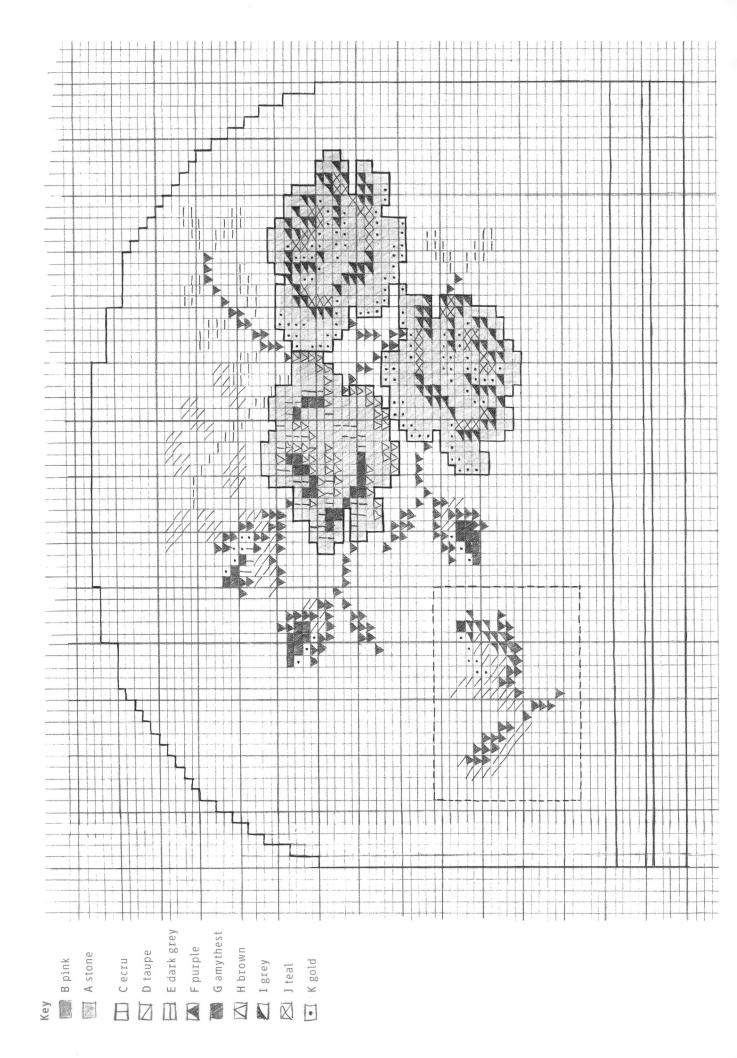

Key

B pink
A stone
C ecru
D taupe
E dark grey
F purple
G amythest
H brown
I grey
J teal
K gold

Work 1 row.
Dec 1 st at each end of next 9 rows. *40 sts*
Cast off 5 sts at beg of next 4 rows. *20 sts*
Work 1 row.
Cast off.

Back

Work as for Front, referring to chart, but working the small bud motif in the dotted box only.
Referring to chart, Swiss darn all other colours over the colour block motifs.

To finish

Weave in any loose yarn ends. *See Masterclass, page 67.*
Lay the work out flat and gently steam the finished piece on the reverse.
Sew all around curved edge, leaving a 1.5cm gap at top.
Fold tape in half, insert into gap and sew into position to make the hanging loop.
Cut pattern for wadding by drawing round work and cut 2 pieces from wadding. Repeat for lining but add 1.5cm seam allowance all round.
Place wadding pieces together and sew around curved edge 1.5 cm inside edge. Do not turn inside out.
With wrong sides of fabric together sew around curved edge 1.5 cm inside edge.
Place unturned out lining inside wadding 'pocket'.
Insert into knitted cosy turn in bottom ends and sew all around hem.

Masterclass

Swiss darning

Swiss darning is a form of embroidery made to look like knit stitches, which is why it is also known as duplicate stitch. Using a tapestry needle and yarn, small areas of colour can be sewn over the top of a knitted stitch to add decorative detail without the tricky technique of knitting with multiple colours. To knit each of the coloured stitches that make up the rose motif on this tea cosy would be incredibly difficult and challenge even the most proficient knitter. I think you will get a far better result by embroidering the odd highlight colour over a base colour. But do make sure when you are Swiss darning over the top of the knitted stitches, not to pull the embroidered stitches too tight as this will pucker the fabric.

1 To work a horizontal row of Swiss darning, work from right to left across the knitted fabric. Bring the needle through from the back of the fabric at the base of a stitch then take it under the two loops at the base of the stitch above.
2 Put the needle back through to the back of the fabric where it first came out at the base of the lower stitch and take it across to come out at the base of the next stitch to the left. One Swiss-darned stitch is complete.

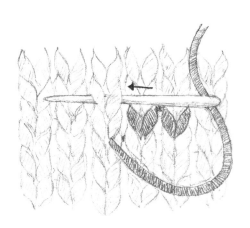

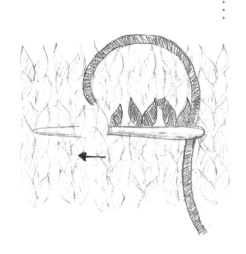

19 V Neck Sweater

A simple sweater knitted in basic stocking stitch with k1, p1 rib details. It will work in most medium weight yarns; here it is made in a soft pima cotton, but would work beautifully in merino, linen or alpaca. The design is classic with a 'v' neck and defined fully fashioned marks to make a feature made by increasing and decreasing, making it a perennial piece.

Skill level...

■ ■ ■ □
EXPERIENCED

In this project you will learn...

Fully fashioned shaping; picking up stitches

Stitches used...

Stocking stitch; k1, p1 rib

Size

To fit (chest)	xs	s	m	l	xl	
	81	86	91	97	102	cm
	32	34	36	38	40	in
Actual (chest)	86	92	97	102	108	cm
	34	36¼	38¼	40¼	42½	in
Length	56	58	60	62	64	cm
	21¾	23	23½	24½	25	in
Sleeve	42	44	46	46	48	cm
	16½	17½	18	18	19	in

Materials
8 x 50g balls of dk-weight yarn, such as
  Rowan Pima Cotton DK (4) MEDIUM
Pair each of 3.25mm and 4mm knitting needles
Large blunt-ended sewing needle

Tension
22 sts and 30 rows to 10cm square measured over stocking stitch using 4mm needles

Notes
Work all the increases and decreases three stitches in from the edges to create a fully fashioned detail.
See Masterclass on page 108.

To make the V Neck Sweater
Back
Using 3.25mm needles cast on 97 (103: 109: 115: 119) sts.
Row 1 (RS) K1, * p1, k1, rep from * to end.
Row 2 * P1, k1, rep from * to last st, p1.
These 2 rows set k1, p1 rib.
Cont in rib until work measures 5cm, ending with WS facing for next row and AT THE SAME TIME dec 1 st at end of last row. *96 (102: 108: 114: 118) sts.*
Change to 4mm needles and cont as folls:
Row 1 (RS) Knit.
Row 2 Purl.
These 2 rows set the stocking stitch.
Cont in st st until back measures 37 (38: 39: 40: 41)cm, ending with a WS row.
Shape armholes
Cast off 5 sts at beg of next 2 rows.
86 (92: 98: 104: 108) sts.
Working dec as above dec 1 st at each end of next 5 rows.
76 (82: 88: 94: 98) sts
Working dec as above dec 1 st at each end of next and and 2 foll alt rows.
70 (76: 82: 88: 92) sts
Cont without shaping until armhole measures 18 (19: 20: 21: 22)cm, ending with RS facing for next row.
Shape shoulders and back neck
Cast off 5 (5: 6: 7: 7) sts at beg of next 2 rows.
60 (66: 70: 74: 78) sts.
Next row Cast off 5 (6: 6: 7: 7) sts, knit until there are 9 (10: 11: 11: 11) sts on the needle, turn and leaving rem sts on a stitch holder cont on these 9 (10: 11: 11: 11) sts.

Next row (WS) Cast off 4 sts, purl to end.
5 (6: 7: 7: 7) sts.
Cast off rem 5 (6: 7: 7: 7) sts.
With RS facing, working on rem sts, leave centre 32 (34: 36: 38: 42) sts on a holder, rejoin yarn to rem 14 (16: 17: 18: 18) sts and knit to end.
Complete to match first side of neck, reversing all shapings.

Front
Work as given for Back to start of armhole shaping, ending with RS facing for next row.
Shape armholes
Cast off 5 sts at beg of next 2 rows.
86 (92: 98: 104: 108) sts.
Working dec as above dec 1 st at each end of next 2 rows.
82 (88: 94: 100: 104) sts.
Shape neck
Working all dec as above cont as folls:
Next row K3, k2tog, knit until there are 35 (38: 41: 43: 46) sts on needle, k2tog tbl, k3, turn and leave rem sts on a holder.
39 (42: 45: 48: 50) sts.
Work 4 rows, dec 1 st at neck edge in 2nd and foll alt row and AT THE SAME TIME dec 1 st at armhole edge in every row.
33 (36: 39: 42: 44) sts.
Work 3 rows, dec 1 st at each end of next and foll alt row.
31 (34: 37: 40: 42) sts.
Dec 1 st at neck edge only in 2nd and every foll alt row to 16 (20: 22: 25: 24) sts then on every foll 4th row to 15 (17: 19: 21: 21) sts.
Cont without shaping until armhole matches back to start of shoulder shaping, ending with RS facing for next row.
With RS facing, rejoin yarn to rem sts, k3, k2tog, knit to last 5 sts, k2tog tbl, k3.
39 (42: 45: 48: 50) sts.
Complete to match first side, reversing all shapings.

Sleeves
Make two the same
Using 3.25mm needles cast on 59 (61: 63: 65: 65) sts.
Work in k1, p1 rib as set on Back cont until work measures 7cm, ending with RS facing for next row.
Change to 4mm needles and beg with a knit row, cont in st st and AT THE SAME TIME inc 1 st at each end of 11th and every foll 20th (16th: 14th: 12th: 10th) row to 69 (73: 77: 81: 85) sts.
Cont until sleeve measures 42 (44: 46: 46: 48)cm, ending with RS facing for next row.
Shape sleeve top
Cast off 5 sts at beg of next 2 rows.
59 (63: 67: 71: 75) sts.
Working decreases as above dec 1 st at each end of next 5 rows, then on every foll alt row until 23 sts rem.
Dec 1 st at each end of next 5 rows. 13 sts.

Neckband
Join right shoulder seam.
With RS facing, using 3.25mm needles pick up and knit 42 (44: 46: 48: 50) sts down left side of neck, place marker on needle, pick up and knit 43 (45: 47: 49: 51) sts up right side of neck, 3 sts down side of back neck, knit across 32 (34: 36: 38: 42) sts from holder at back neck, and pick up and knit 4 sts up side of back neck.
125 (131: 137: 143: 151) sts.
Starting with 2nd row of rib as set on Back cont as folls:
Row 1 (WS) P1, *k1, p1, rep to marker, move marker to right needle, p1, * k1, p1, rep to end.
Row 2 Rib as set to 2 sts before marker, k2tog tbl, slip marker to right needle, k2tog, rib to end.
Row 3 Rib as set to 2 sts before marker, p2tog, slip marker to right needle, p2tog tbl, rib to end.
Rep last 2 rows until neckband measures 2.5cm.
Cast off in rib.

To finish
Join left shoulder and neckband seam. Set in sleeves with an invisible seam from the right side. Join side and sleeve seams with an invisible seam from the right side.
Weave in any loose yarn ends. *See Masterclass, page 67.*
Lay the work out flat and gently steam the finished piece on the reverse.

Masterclass

Picking up stitches along a neck edge

A well knitted neckband to a sweater can
really make a garment. It is possible to knit a
neckband separately and then sew it in place
but I prefer to pick up stitches around the
neck edge and knit on the neckband.

To ensure that your neckband is knitted
evenly all round the neck edge, before you
start picking up stitches divide the area into
even sections and mark each with a pin or
contrast colour yarn. Divide the number of
stitches for be picked up by the number of
sections marked out and that is the number of
stitches to be picked up in each section. For
example, if you need to pick up 48 stitches
are you have divided your neck edge up into 8
sections, then you need to pick up 6 stitches in
each section. I find it far easier to pick up 6
stitches evenly over a small area than it is to
judge 48 stitches over an entire neck edge.

From the front of the fabric, put the tip
of a knitting needle into the space between
the edge stitch and the next stitch. Wrap the
working yarn around the needle. Bring the
needle and the working yarn through to the
front of the work. Continue in this way until
the required numbers of stitches have been
picked up.

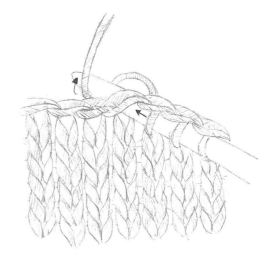

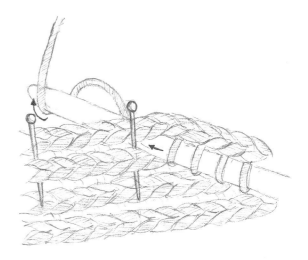

Pocket Cardigan

A timeless cardigan knitted in luxuriously soft baby alpaca yarn with a deep v neck, integral button bands and 'fashioned' pockets. Trimmed with linen tape in the back neck and fastened with mother of-pearl buttons, this a truly classic garment.

Skill level...

EXPERIENCED

In this project you will learn...

Knitting in patch pockets

Stitches used...

Stocking stitch

Size

To fit (chest)	xs	s	m	l	xl	
	81	86	91	97	102	cm
	32	34	36	38	40	in
Actual (chest)	86	92	97	102	108	cm
	34	36¼	38¼	40¼	42½	in
Length	65	67	69	71	73	cm
	25½	26½	27¼	28	28¾	in
Sleeve	42	44	46	46	48	cm
	16½	17½	18	18	19	in

Materials

12 (13: 13: 14: 15) x 50g balls dk weight wool yarn, such as Rowan Baby Alpaca DK (4) MEDIUM
Pair each of 3.25mm and 4mm knitting needles
4 x 5mm diameter buttons
Large blunt-ended sewing needle

Tension

22 stitches and 30 rows to 10cm square measued over stocking stitch using 4mm needles

To make the Cardigan
Back
Using 3.25mm needles cast on 97 (103: 109: 115: 119) sts.
Row 1 (RS) K1, * p1, k1, rep from * to end.
Row 2 * P1, k1, rep from * to last st, p1.
These 2 rows set k1, p1 rib.
Work 14 rows more in rib as set, ending with RS facing for next row.
Change to 4mm needles and beg with a knit row work in stocking stitch – knit one row and purl one row alternately – until work measures 46 (47: 48: 49: 50)cm, ending with RS facing for next row.
Shape armholes
Cast off 5 sts at beg of next 2 rows. *87 (93: 99: 105: 109) sts.*
Working dec as above dec 1 st at each end of next 5 rows. *77 (83: 89: 95: 99) sts.*
Working dec as above dec 1 st at each end of next and and 2 foll alt rows. *71 (77: 83: 89: 93) sts.*
Cont without shaping until armhole measures 18 (19: 20: 21: 22)cm, ending with RS facing for next row.
Shape shoulders and back neck
Cast off 5 (6: 7: 8: 8) sts at beg of next 2 rows. *61 (65: 69: 73: 77) sts.*
Next row Cast off 5 (6: 7: 8: 8) sts, knit until there are 10 (11: 11: 12: 13) sts on the needle, turn and leaving rem sts on a stitch holder cont on these 10 (11: 11: 12: 13) sts.
Next row (WS) Cast off 4 sts, purl to end. *6 (7: 7: 8: 9) sts.*
Cast off rem 6 (7: 7: 8: 9) sts.
With RS facing, working on rem sts, cast off centre 31 (31: 33: 33: 35) sts, rejoin yarn to rem 15 (17: 18: 20: 21) sts and knit to end.
Next row (WS) Cast off 5 (6: 7: 8: 8) sts, purl to end. *10 (11: 11: 12: 13) sts.*
Next row Cast off 4 sts, knit to end. *6 (7: 7: 8: 9) sts.*
Cast off rem 6 (7: 7: 8: 9) sts.

Pocket linings
Make two the same
Using 4mm needles cast on 29 sts and beg with a knit row work 14cm stocking stitch, ending with RS facing for next row.
Next row Dec 1 st at each end of next row. 27 sts.
Leave stitches on a holder.

Left front
Using 3.25mm needles cast on 53 (57: 59: 63: 65) sts.
Work 16 rows in rib as set on Back, ending with RS facing for next row.

Change to 4mm needles and work as follows:
Row 1 (RS) Knit to last 12 sts, rib as set to end.
Row 2 Rib first 12 sts as set, purl to end.
Rep these 2 rows until work measures 16cm from cast on edge, ending with RS facing for next row. Work pocket top as folls:
Next row K6 [10:12:16:18] sts, (k1, p1) 13 times, knit to last 12 sts, rib 12 as set.
Next row Rib 12, p9, rib 27 as set, p6 (10: 12: 16: 18) sts.
Rep last 2 rows three times more.
Next row K6 (10: 12: 16: 18), cast off next 27 sts in rib, work to end.
Next row Rib 12, p9, with WS of pocket facing p27 sts from one holder, work to end of row. *53 (57: 59: 63: 65) sts.*
Pocket lining is now part of the cardigan front. Cont straight with rib edging as set until work measures 36 (37: 38: 39: 50)cm from cast-on edge, ending with RS facing for next row.
Shape front slope
Next row (dec) Work to last 17 sts, k2tog tbl, k3, rib 12.
Next row Rib 12, work to end of row.
Working dec as set above dec 1 st at neck edge in following 3rd and 4 following 6th rows. *47 (51: 53: 57: 59) sts.*
Work 1 row, ending with RS facing for next row.
Front now matches Back to start of armhole shaping.
Shape armhole
Next row Cast off 5 sts, knit to end. *42 (46: 48: 52: 54) sts.*
Next row Purl.
Working dec as set above dec 1 st at armhole edge in next 5 rows, then on 3 foll alt rows AT SAME TIME dec 1 st at neck edge in 5th row. *33 (37: 39: 43: 45) sts.*
Keeping armhole straight, continue to dec at front edge in 3rd and every foll 6th row until 30 (33: 36: 36: 37) sts remain.
For 1st, 2nd and 3rd sizes only
Dec 1 st at neck edge in every foll 8th row to 28 (31: 33) sts.
For all 5 sizes
Cont without shaping until armhole matches back to start of shoulder shaping, ending with RS facing for next row.
Next row Cast off 5 (6: 7: 8: 8) sts and work to last 12 sts, turn, leaving the 12 rib sts on a holder. *11 [13: 14: 16: 17] sts.*
Work 1 row.
Cast off 5 [6: 7: 8: 8] sts at beg of next row. *6 (7:*

7: 8: 9) sts.
Work 1 row.
Cast off rem 6 [7: 7: 8: 9] sts.

Right front
Using 3.25mm needles cast on 53 (57: 59: 63: 65) sts.
Work 8 rows in rib as set on Back.
Buttonhole row 1 (RS) Rib 5 sts, cast off next 2 sts, rib to end.
Buttonhole row 2 Rib as set, casting on 2 sts over the sts cast off on row 1.
Work a further 6 rows in rib, ending with RS facing for next row.
Change to 4mm needles and work as follows, working 4 more buttonholes at 8.5cm intervals:
Row 1 (RS) Rib 12 sts as set, knit to end.
Row 2 Purl to last 12 sts, rib as set.
Rep last 2 rows until work measures 16cm from cast-on edge ending with RS facing for next row. Don't forget the buttonholes.
Work pocket top as follows:
Next row Rib 12, k9, (k1, p1) 13 times, knit to end.
Next row P6 (10: 12: 16: 18), rib 27 as set, p9, rib 12.
Repeat last 2 rows three times more.
Next row Rib 12, k9, cast off next 27 sts in rib, work to end.
Next row P6 (10: 12: 16: 18), then with WS of pocket lining facing, p27 sts from holder, purl to last 12 sts, rib as set. *53 (57: 59: 63: 65) sts.*
Pocket lining is now part of the cardigan front. Cont straight with rib edging as set until work measures 36 (37: 38: 39: 50)cm from cast-on edge, ending RS facing for next row.
Shape front slope
Next row (dec) Rib 12, k3, k2tog, knit to end.
Next row Purl to last 12 stitches, rib 12.
Working dec as set above dec 1 st at neck edge (as above) on following 3rd and 4 following 6th rows. *47 (51: 53: 57: 59) sts.*
Work 2 rows, ending with WS facing for next row. (Front should now match Back to start of armhole shaping.)
Shape armhole
Next row (WS) Cast off 5 sts at beg of next row. *42 (46: 48: 52: 54) sts.*
Working dec 1 st as set above dec 1 st as set at neck edge in 5th row AT SAME TIME dec 1 st at armhole edge in next 5 rows, then on 3 foll alt rows. *33 (37: 39: 43: 45) sts.*
Keeping armhole straight, continue to decrease at front edge in 3rd and every foll 6th row until 30 (33: 36: 36: 37) sts remain.

For 1st, 2nd and 3rd sizes only
Decrease 1 st at neck edge in every foll 8th row
to 28 (31: 33) sts.
For all sizes
Cont without shaping until armhole matches back
to start of shoulder shaping, ending with WS
facing for next row.
Next row Cast off 5 (6: 7: 8: 8) sts and work to
last 12 sts, turn, leaving the 12 rib stitches on a
holder. *11 (13: 14: 16: 17) sts.*
Work 1 row.
Cast off 5 (6: 7: 8: 8) sts at beg of next row.
6 (7: 7: 8: 9) sts.
Work 1 row.
Cast off remaining 6 (7: 7: 8: 9) sts.

Sleeves
Make two the same
Using 3.25mm needles cast on 59 (61: 63: 65: 65) sts.
Work in k1, p1 rib as set on Back cont until work
measures 7cm, ending with RS facing for next row.
Change to 4mm needles and starting with a K row,
cont in st st and AT SAME TIME inc 1 st at each
end of 11th and every foll 20th (16th: 14th: 12th:
10th) row to 69 (73: 77: 81: 85) sts.
Cont until sleeve measures 42 (44: 46: 46: 48)cm,
ending with RS facing for next row.
Shape sleeve top
Cast off 5 sts at beg of next 2 rows. *59 (63: 67: 71:
75) sts.*
Working decreases as above, dec 1 st at each end
of next 5 rows, then on every foll alt row until
23 sts rem.
Dec 1 st at each end of next 5 rows. *13 sts.*

To finish
Weave in any loose yarn ends. *See Masterclass,
page 67.*
Gently steam work on reverse.
Join both shoulder seams.
Back neckband
Using 4mm needles and RS of work facing slip
12 sts of right front band onto needle, rejoin
yarn and continue in rib as set until band when
slightly stretched, reaches centre back. Leave
stitches on holder. Repeat for the left front band.
Graft 2 sets of stitches together – need to give
instructions for this.
Sew pocket linings to inside.
Set in sleeves.
Join side and sleeve seams.
Sew on buttons to match buttonholes.

Masterclass

Pockets
There are several different designs of pockets
that can be knitted into garments, depending
on how much of a feature you want them to
be. With this cardigan, I have plumped for a
discreet inset pocket with a ribbed top as it is
neater than a patch pocket.

Recommended yarns

There is a yarn specified for each of the twenty designs in the Project Workshops section of this book. You can stick to the recommended yarn, if so you just need to pick your preferred shade. However, if you want to use a different yarn to the one specified you need to compare the tensions given to ensure the finished result will not differ too wildly.

There are standard weights – or thicknesses – of yarns, recognised throughout the spinner's industry. Handknit yarns commonly range from 4ply (fingering) through double knitting (sport weight) to super bulky at the opposite end of the scale. Within each of these categories there is a degree of tolerance, so it is still important to check the tension of each yarn against that given in a pattern (see Tension, pages 36–7).

Each yarn will have slightly varying physical properties from the next and will perform differently. Some yarns may be colourfast and easycare whilst others may only be suitable for drycleaning or could possibly felt if not treated correctly (see Aftercare, page 47). The care information for a yarn will be given on the ball band that comes wrapped around a ball, hank or skein. I always keep a ball band for each project that I make – and if I give a handknit as a gift, I include the ball band so the recipient knows how to care for the item. When you invest so much of your time and energy into creating a hand-knitted item, great care should be taken in the laundering.

Alongside the manufacturer's brand name and the name given to the specific yarn, a ball band will typically carry the following information:

Average tension and recommended needle sizes
This is the spinner's recommended tension and needle size, however a designer may vary from this recommendation within a pattern. If so, always go with the designer's recommendation.

Weight of yarn
Given in grams in the UK and ounces in the US, most yarns come in either 50g or 100g balls.

Meterage
This is the approximate length of yarn in the ball and is just as important to consider as tension when considering a substitute yarn.

Fibre composition
A ball band will list the materials that the yarn is made from, whether that is 100% pure wool or a blend of fibres such as cotton and silk. This affects not just the method of care for the finished item, but also the suitability of a yarn for a certain project.

Shade and dye lot numbers
Each shade of yarn is given an identifying name and/or number by the manufacturer. When purchasing yarn the dye lot numer is equally, if not more important, as this number needs to be the same on every ball. As yarn is dyed in batches, buying yarn with the same dye lot numbers ensures there will be no colour variations between balls.

Care instructions
A ball band will indicate whether the yarn is suitable for machine washing or is dry clean only, and whether or not it can be iron and, if so, at what temperature. This information is usually given in the form of standard care symbols.

Alchemy Yarns Silk Straw
A dk silk yarn; 100% silk; 215m per 40g; tension – 24 sts per 10cm over st st using 3.5mm needles.

Blue Sky Alpacas Royal Alpaca
A dk alpaca yarn; 100% alpaca; 263m per 100g; tension – 24–28 sts per 10cm over st st using 2.75–3.25mm needles.

Blue Sky Alpacas Worsted Hand Dyes
An aran alpaca yarn; 50% alpaca, 50% merino; 91m per 100g; tension – 16 sts per 10cm over st st using 5.5mm needles.

Debbie Bliss Como
A super chunky wool blend yarn; 90% wool, 10% cashmere; 42m per 50g; tension – 10 sts x 15 rows per 10cm over st st using 10mm needles.

Debbie Bliss Eco Fairtrade Cotton
An aran cotton yarn; 100% cotton; 90m per 50g; tension – 18 sts x 24 rows per 10cm over st st using 4.5mm needles.

Habu Cotton Gima
A super fine cotton yarn; 100% cotton; 236m per 28g; tension – 36 sts x 48 rows per 10cm over st st using 2.25–3.25mm needles.

Habu Silk Gima
A fine silk yarn; 100% silk; 236m per 28g; tension – 26 sts x 36 rows per 10cm over st st using 2.25–3.25mm needles.

Jarol King Dishcloth Cotton
A dk cotton yarn; 100% cotton; tension – 20 sts x 32 rows per 10cm over st st using 4.5mm needles.

Regia Erika Knight Design Line 4ply
A 4ply wool blend yarn; 75% wool, 25% polyamide; 115m per 50g; tension – 30 sts x 12 rows per 10cm over st st using 2.75mm needles.

Rowan Big Wool
A super chunky wool yarn; 100% merino; 80m per 50g; tension – 7.5 x 9 rows per 10cm over st st using 10 or 15mm needles.

Rowan Purelife British Sheeps Breed DK
A dk wool yarn; 100% wool; 120m per 50g ball; tension – 22 sts x 30 rows per 10cm over st st using 4mm needles.

Rowan Cashsoft Aran
An aran merino blend yarn; 57% merino, 33% acrylic microfibre, 10% cashmere; 87m per 50g; tension – 19 sts x 25 rows per 10cm over st st using 4.5mm needles.

Rowan Cashsoft DK
An dk merino blend yarn; 57% merino, 33% acrylic microfibre, 10% cashmere; 130m per 50g; tension – 22 sts x 30 rows per 10cm over st st using 4mm needles.

Rowan Classic Baby Alpaca DK
A dk alpaca yarn; 100% baby alpaca; 100m per 50g; tension – 22 sts x 30 rows per 10cm over st st using 4mm needles.

Rowan Kidsilk Aura
A dk mohair blend; 75% kidsilk mohair, 25% silk; 75m per 25g; tension – 16–20 sts x 19–28 rows per 10cm over st st using 4–6mm needles.

Rowan Lenpur Linen
A dk linen blend yarn; 75% VI Lenpur, 25% linen; 115m per 50g; tension – 22 sts x 30 rows per 10cm over st st using 4mm needles.

Rowan Pima Cotton DK
A dk cotton yarn; 100% pima cotton; 130m per 50g; tension – 22 sts x 30 rows per 10cm over st st using 4mm needles.

Rowan Pure Silk DK
A dk silk yarn; 100% silk; 125m per 50g; tension – 22 sts x 30 rows per 10cm over st st using 4mm needles.

Yeoman's Cotton Cannele 4ply
A 4ply cotton yarn; 100% mercerised cotton; 850m per 245g cone; tension – 33 sts x 44 rows per 10cm over st st using 2.75mm needles.

Needle Sizes
There are three systems of sizing needles. The most commonly used system in the UK and Europe is metric, in which needle sizes are given in millimetres. The other two systems are US standard and the older UK and Canadian imperial. The chart below gives the equivalent sizes across all three systems.

Metric	US	Imperial
25	50	–
19	35	–
15	19	–
10	15	000
9	13	00
8	11	0
7.5	11	1
7	10½	2
6.5	10½	3
6	10	4
5.5	9	5
5	8	6
4.5	7	7
4	6	8
3.75	5	9
3.5	4	–
3.25	3	10
3	2/3	11
2.75	2	12
2.25	1	13
2	0	14
1.75	00	–
1.5	000	–

Acknowledgements

In spite of its simple title and ethos this has been a complex book to put together. It has involved the very best people of the highest calibre with the most discerning eyes, exacting standards, meticulous attention to detail and above all unbelievable patience, for which I am enormously grateful and I would like to extend my heartfelt appreciation for their huge contributions. It is a privilege to work with them and certainly this book would not have happened without them.

The truly wonderful team at Quadrille. To my Editorial Director, and indeed mentor, Jane O'Shea. To my project editor Lisa Pendreigh – my sincerest thanks for her professionalism, exceptional expertise, patience and personal support – as well as designer Claire Peters for her emphatic and creative design. And Ruth Deary for doing such a fabulous job in the production of the book.

It has been fabulous to have Yuki Sugiura photograph this book; her ease, empathy and natural sense of style is central to the sensibility of this book. And, of course, Lara for assisting and for all things culinary and cool. My thanks, too, to our stylist Charis, for her diligence in the detail; she always had it there.

To my brilliant project maker, problem solver and personal friend Sally Lee, enormously grateful for her misspent or rather well spent youth crafting, knitting, sewing and making stuff, all which has paid off. To Sarah Hatton for gracing this book with her expertise and presence and Eileen Bundie for knitting par excellence. And of course technically Gina Alton, for her inestimable and meticulous work in pattern checking. Thanks too to Ian Harris for his wise, succinct and supportive critique.

As people who know me will testify, I pour over all the detail all the time, but the selection of yarn is paramount to me and most especially when designing and offering projects of simple design. Hence my sincerest thanks and appreciation to the following createurs of exceptional yarns of rare distinction for their generosity and enthusiastic support. As always the iconic yarn brand of Rowan, Regia, Habu, Gina Wilde of Alchemy, Blue Sky Alpacas, Debbie Bliss Designer yarns and Yeoman's Yarns for constantly producing desirable fibres and yarns of excellent quality which entice and excite the creative soul. Long may you continue to do so.

Finally this book is dedicated to creatives and crafters everywhere, especially to the new breed of artisan entrepreneurs who are emerging and growing in number and confidence: who continually excite with their passion for the hand made, who constantly push the boundaries of craft with their enthusiasm, innovation and origination. The future is yours!

Publisher's Acknowledgements
The publisher would like to thank the following for loaning accessories and other items:

THE ISLE MILL
Macnaughton Holdings Ltd, Tower House, Ruthvenfield Road, Perth PH1 3UN
Tel: 01738-609090

ERCOL
Summerleys Road, Princes Risborough, Buckinghamshire HP27 9PX
Tel: 01844-271800

FANNY'S ANTIQUES
1 Lynmouth Road, Reading, Berkshire RG1 8DE
Tel: 0118 950 8261